100 GREATEST
BASKETBALL
PLAYERS

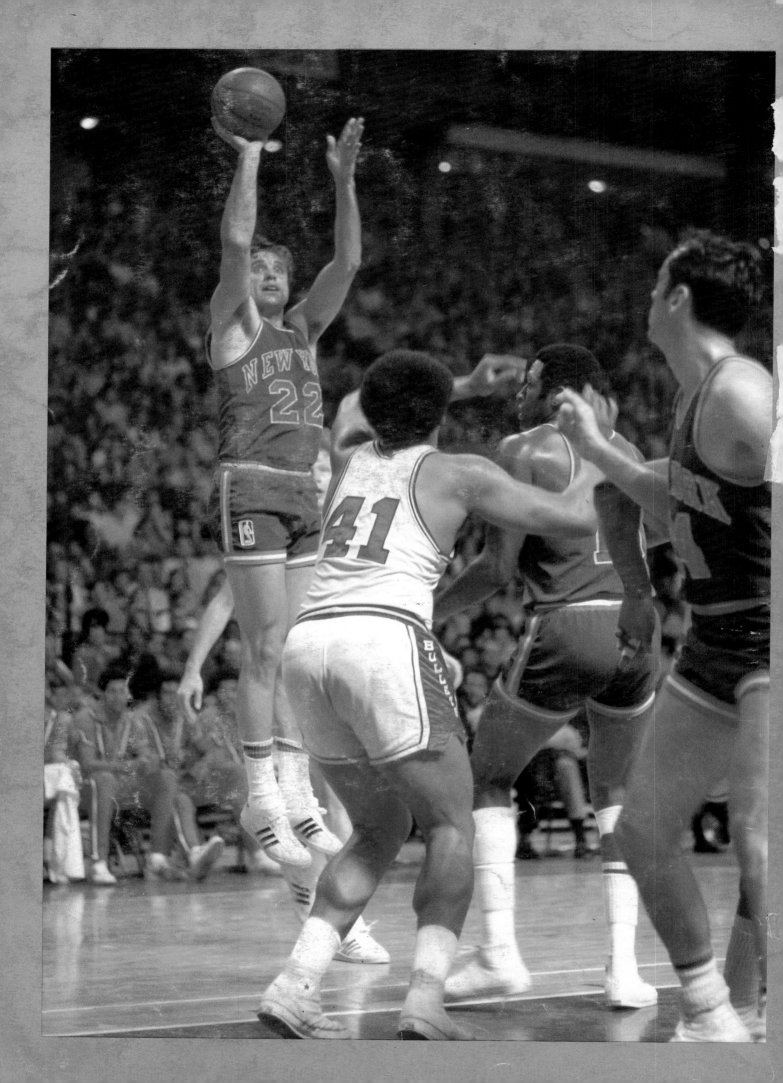

100 GREATEST BASKETBALL PLAYERS

Wayne Patterson
and
Lisa Fisher

Crescent Books
A Division of Crown Publishers, Inc.

Page 1: A classic matchup: Wilt Chamberlain versus Bill Russell, 24 March 1960.

Page 2: Jerry Lucas averaged 17.0 points and 15.6 boards per game in 11 NBA seasons.

Left: Elgin Baylor's fluid drives were tough to defend.

The 1989 edition published by Crescent Books, distributed by Crown Publishers, Inc. 225 Park Avenue South New York, NY 10003

Produced by Brompton Books Corp. 15 Sherwood Place Greenwich, CT 06830

Library of Congress Cataloguing-in-Publication Data
Patterson, Wayne and Lisa Fisher.
  100 greatest basketball players.
    p.   cm.
  Includes index.
  1. Basketball players—United States—Biography. 2. Women basketball players—United States—Biography. 3. Basketball players—United States—Pictorial works. I. Crescent Books. II. Title: One hundred greatest basketball players.
GV884.A1A15   1989
796.323'092'2—dc20   89-7652
[B]   CIP

ISBN 0-517-67731-8

h g f e d c b

Printed in Hong Kong

Acknowledgments

The authors would like to thank John Bowman, for giving us the chance to write this book; Mr. Joe O'Brien, Executive Director of the Naismith Memorial Basketball Hall of Fame; and Jerry Healy and Jim Mullen, for their assistance. Wayne Patterson would like to thank his wife, Kelly, for all her patience and understanding. Thanks also go to the following people who helped in the preparation of this book: Mike Rose, designer; Jean Martin, editor; Rita Longabucco, picture editor; and Florence Norton, indexer.

Picture Credits

The Bettmann Archive: 52, 92(top).
Malcolm Emmons: 2, 4, 6(left), 7, 8(left), 10(left), 11(bottom), 12, 14(both), 15, 16(bottom), 17, 18(both), 22(all three), 23, 24, 25(top), 28, 29(bottom), 30, 31(all three), 37(both), 40(both), 44(right), 45, 47, 50(top, bottom left), 51(both), 53, 54, 55(top), 57(bottom), 58(both), 59(bottom), 60(both), 62, 63(bottom left, bottom right), 64, 65(bottom), 67(left), 71(both), 72, 73(top), 75(left), 76(both), 80, 81(left), 82, 87(both), 88(both), 89, 90(bottom), 97(top left, top right), 100(right), 101, 102(bottom left), 103, 104(bottom), 105, 107, 108(both), 109, 111.
Nancy Hogue: 6(right), 8(right), 10(right), 12(bottom), 19, 29(top), 36, 44(left), 50(bottom right), 55(bottom), 56, 70, 74, 77, 81(right), 85, 96, 99, 100(left), 102(top, bottom right), 104(top), 106(both).
Naismith Memorial Basketball Hall of Fame/The Edward J. & Gena G. Hickox Library: 9, 11(top), 12(top), 16(top), 20, 21(both), 25(bottom), 32, 34, 35, 41, 42, 43, 46, 48, 49, 57(top), 63(top), 65(top), 66, 69, 73(bottom), 75(right), 78, 79, 83, 84(both), 90(top), 91, 93, 95, 97, 97(bottom).
UPI/Bettmann Newsphotos: 1, 26, 27, 33, 38, 39, 59(top), 61, 67(right), 68, 86, 92(bottom), 98.

INTRODUCTION

Basketball – 'The American Game Played Worldwide.' This best describes the game that Dr. James Naismith invented in 1891. Since that cold December day in Springfield, Massachusetts, the game of basketball has been played by millions of men and women around the world.

Basketball, unlike any other team sport, can be practiced alone. A player can rehearse the moves, practice dribbling and improve a shot by himself, with only a basket and a ball. This sequence is played out by youngsters across the country in gymnasiums, parks, and driveways. The dream of every young basketball player is to sink the basket that will win a championship. Each player in this book has sweated through hours and hours of solitary practice. There are stories about a young Pete Maravich or a young Michael Jordan spending hour after hour, day after day, in any kind of weather, throwing a ball through a hoop. This kind of dedication makes superstars.

However, compiling a list of the 100 greatest athletes ever to play basketball is difficult and bound to provoke controversy. There have been great high school players, great college players and professional superstars. How do you single out only 100? This is not a list of the 100 greatest centers or the 100 greatest shooters. This is a list of the 100 greatest overall players. We have had the unenviable task of comparing guards to centers, of comparing a player who played before the inception of the shot clock to a player of today.

We put every reasonable candidate on a list and narrowed it down to what we thought to be the 100 greatest basketball players of all time. Not only did we have to pick the 100 greatest players, we also had to rate them according to greatness. This job was difficult, but proved to be challenging and fun.

Our top criteria in defining greatness are statistics. Basketball is a game of statistics. The authors know that the bottom line of any sport is winning or losing. However, we are not doing a team book – we are creating a list of the greatest individuals ever to don a basketball uniform. When you speak of individuals, you speak of statistics. Ultimately, statistics lead to individual awards, i.e. Most Valuable Player, leading scorer in league, etc. The greatest players in the history of basketball have many outstanding individual achievements to their credit.

We also know that statistics are only one of the criteria in defining greatness. Leadership and team success must be viewed as well. These two components do not carry as much weight as statistics, but must be considered.

When anyone talks of the greatest player in basketball history, there are three names that always come to mind: Wilt Chamberlain, Bill Russell, and Kareem Abdul-Jabbar. Each of them has given something different to the world of basketball. The opinion of the authors is that Wilt

Chamberlain is the greatest basketball player of all time. Upon his retirement, Wilt's individual accomplishments stood in a league by themselves. He even set a few records that might never be equaled. True, Bill Russell helped his teams to two NCAA Championships and 11 NBA World Championships, and Kareem Abdul-Jabbar broke many of Chamberlain's records, including the most career points in the NBA. The argument as to who is the greatest will never be settled, but to us, Wilt Chamberlain's accomplishments stand out above the rest.

We also chose to include two women in the book, to show that there is a place in basketball history for women. These two individuals are the reason why women's basketball is on the upswing. There are many other women we would like to have included in the list, but Nancy Lieberman and Ann Meyers are the cream of the crop when it comes to women's basketball.

We hope you have as much fun reading the book as we had putting it together. The compilation of the list depended on a lot of hard work and effort by many people and we are indebted to all of them.

Top left: *With his shooting touch and deft passing, Oscar Robertson could take over a game – and did for 14 years in the NBA.*

Top right: *Pete Maravich, the ultimate showman, dazzled crowds with his dribbling, fancy passing, and shots from downtown.*

Opposite: *Kareem Abdul-Jabbar is the NBA's all-time leading scorer.*

Kareem Abdul-Jabbar

It was the night of 5 April 1984 in Las Vegas and the Los Angeles Lakers were playing the Utah Jazz. The Lakers' great center, Kareem Abdul-Jabbar, was closing in on Wilt Chamberlain's scoring record (31,419 career points). In that game, near the end of the third quarter, Kareem put up one of his famous sky hooks and passed Chamberlain to become the NBA's all-time leading scorer.

During his three-year college career, UCLA went 88-2 and the Bruins won three consecutive national titles. The three-time All-American averaged 26.4

points per game, and was the College Player-of-the-Year in 1967 and 1969. He was named the NCAA Tournament Most Outstanding Player all three years. Known as Lew Alcindor in high school and college, Kareem was drafted by the Milwaukee Bucks with the first pick of the draft. The Rookie-of-the Year immediately turned the Bucks into a playoff contender, and the team won the World Championship in 1971, his second year.

In one of the most amazing trades in NBA history, the Bucks sent Kareem to the Los Angeles Lakers for four players. He led the Lakers to five World Championships and is one of 15 players who have won a title with two different NBA teams. He has earned many individual honors by being named to the All-NBA First Team ten times, named the NBA's MVP six times (the most by any NBA player), named to the All-NBA Defensive First Team five times, and named the NBA Playoff MVP twice. Kareem has led the league in scoring twice, rebounding once, field goal percentage once, and blocked shots four times.

The 7 ft 2 in center holds many NBA season records as well. In 1988, he entered his 20th and last season. He has played more games (1486) and minutes (55,751) than any other player. Along with the scoring record of 37,639 points, Kareem has 15,524 field goals made, 27,648 attempted, and 3104 blocked shots. In 17 NBA All-Star game appearances, he has played the most minutes (436), has the most field goals attempted (207) and field goals made (104), and is first on the All-Star career scoring list with 247. Just about the only thing he has not done is win an All-Star game MVP.

Mark Aguirre

Mark Aguirre averaged 24.5 points per game in three years at DePaul University in Chicago, Illinois. The two-time All-American was the 1981 College Player-of-the-Year. He was a member of the 1980 U.S. Olympic team, which did not get a chance to play in the games.

The 6 ft 6 in forward was drafted as an undergraduate by the Dallas Mavericks as the number one pick of the 1981 draft. In his playing career with the Mavericks, he has averaged 24.9 points per game. Aguirre led Dallas to the playoffs five consecutive times, and was the first Maverick to play in an NBA All-Star game. He is the team's all-time leading scorer with 12,977 points, and has the 11th highest scoring average in NBA history.

In 1989, Aguirre was traded to Detroit for Adrian Dantley. Aguirre is a consistent player who is a scoring threat at all times.

Opposite: *For 20 seasons, Kareem's sky hook devastated the NBA and helped him earn six MVP awards. A finesse player, Jabbar could bring the ball up court if necessary.*

Right: *Averaging 24.9 points per game makes Mark Aguirre an All-Star and the main man in the Dallas offense.*

Nate Archibald

In his magical year of 1973, Nate Archibald of the Kansas City-Omaha Kings did something that no other player had ever done – he led the NBA in scoring and assists in the same season. The 6 ft 1 in point guard was drafted out of Texas-El Paso by the Cincinnati Royals in the second round of the 1970 draft (19th overall). The best penetrating guard in NBA history played 14 seasons, though often plagued by injury, with seven different teams. He took part in six NBA All-Star games and was named game MVP in 1981 when he scored nine points and had nine assists.

In 1978 he went to the Boston Celtics in a blockbuster trade that included nine players. 'Tiny,' the most prolific scoring and passing guard in the league, helped rebuild the Celtics to become a powerhouse team of the 1980s. In 1981 he led them to a championship season, averaging 15.6 points and 6.1 assists in the playoffs.

Archibald ended his 14-year career with 16,481 points (31st on the all-time list) and 6476 assists (sixth on the all-time list). He had a career-high 23 assists in one game in 1979, the seventh best in NBA history.

Above: *A slashing guard, Nate Archibald led the NBA in scoring and assists in 1973.*

Right: *'Tiny' dished off for 6476 career assists – sixth on the all-time list.*

Paul Arizin

Paul Arizin is 'Philadelphia's Pride,' having grown up and played his entire basketball career in Pennsylvania. He led the NCAA Division I in scoring with 735 points in 1950 at Villanova University. He was a unanimous choice as All-American and College Player-of-the-Year.

The 6 ft 4 in forward was drafted by the Philadelphia Warriors. In ten seasons, all with the Warriors, 'Pitchin' Paul' was one of the NBA's most consistent scorers, leading the league in 1952 and 1957. He was selected to play in nine NBA All-Star games and was named game MVP in 1952.

During his career, Paul scored 16,266 points (32nd on the all-time list) and led Philadelphia to eight playoff appearances, winning one Championship in 1956. Known as the craftsman of the jump shot, he revolutionized the game with his tremendous shooting accuracy. For three seasons he played with Wilt Chamberlain, and in 1961-62 they combined to average 72.3 points. No other two teammates have ever accomplished this.

Paul's basketball career culminated in his election to the NBA 25th Anniversary All-Time Team and enshrinement at the Basketball Hall of Fame.

Charles Barkley

At Auburn University, Charles Barkley averaged 14.1 points and 9.6 rebounds per game. With the fifth pick of the first round, the Philadelphia 76ers drafted him as an undergraduate in 1984. After four NBA seasons, all with the 76ers, Barkley has averaged 21.2 points per game. The 6 ft 6 in forward was named to the All-NBA Rookie Team, named to the All-NBA Second Team twice, named to the All-NBA First Team once, and is a three-time recipient of the Schick Pivotal Player Award. He has played in two All-NBA Star games and has scored an average of 20.6 points per game in 30 playoff games.

Barkley is the shortest player since Harry Gallatin (1954) to lead the league in rebounding. 'The Round Mound of Rebound' accomplished this in 1987 with an average of 14.6 rebounds per game. At 6 ft 6 in and 263 pounds, Barkley is built like a tank and is famous for his end-to-end runs which usually are completed with a ferocious dunk.

Top: *Paul Arizin, an NBA sharpshooter for 10 seasons.*

Right: *Charles Barkley led the NBA with 14.6 boards per game in 1987.*

Tom Barlow

Tom Barlow was born in Trenton, New Jersey and was graduated from Ride Moore Stewart Business College. He turned professional at the age of 16 and played outstanding ball throughout the East. The 6 ft 1 in guard attained stardom for 20 years (1912-32) with various league teams. He played for Trenton in the Eastern League, DeNeri in the Metropolitan League, and Wilmington and the SPHAs in the Philadelphia League. From 1926 to 1932, Barlow played with the Philadelphia Warriors in the American Basketball League and was team captain of Hagerstown, Maryland; Pottsville, Pennsylvania; and Union City, the Trenton Marshall's, the Laurels and the Tigers in New Jersey.

'Babe' played in the first professional game held at New York's Madison Square Garden. A strong, popular player, a fine scorer and outstanding defender, he was considered one of the very best players of his era, when the professional game barnstormed across the Northeast to Illinois.

Rick Barry

The only player to lead the NCAA, ABA, and NBA in scoring is Rick Barry. He completed a successful college career at the University of Miami by leading the NCAA in scoring with a 37.4 average in 1965.

The 6 ft 7 in forward was drafted fourth by the San Francisco Warriors and went on to a brilliant 14-year career divided between the NBA and ABA. After his first season he was named NBA Rookie-of-the-Year, and he followed that up by leading the NBA in scoring in his second year. Following four years in the ABA, the greatest shooting forward of all time returned to the NBA. He played in seven NBA All-Star games and was named game MVP in 1967.

During his career, Rick scored 18,395 points (20th on the all-time list) and led the Golden State Warriors to an NBA Championship in 1975. He is co-holder of the record for the most three-point field goals in a game with eight and is the all-time leader in free throw percentage with a career average of .900. One of his distinctions was that he shot his free throws underhanded. Barry closed out his remarkable career by being enshrined at the Basketball Hall of Fame.

Top: *Tom Barlow.*

Right: *Rick Barry's career 90 percent free throw accuracy is tops.*

Opposite: *During 14 seasons Barry rained jump shots from all over and scored 18,395 points.*

Elgin Baylor

Elgin Baylor is widely recognized as one of the greatest scoring forwards in basketball history. He is considered one of the first all-around players in the game. He could do everything – shoot, pass, rebound, score, and play defense.

While at Seattle University, he led the NCAA Division I in rebounding. The 6 ft 5 in forward was drafted in the first round by the Minneapolis Lakers in 1958. In 14 seasons, all with the Lakers (two in Minneapolis, 12 in Los Angeles), he led them to the NBA Finals eight times, although they never did take the championship.

During his career, Elgin scored 23,149 points (seventh on the all-time list) in the regular season and 3623 points (fourth on the all-time list) in the playoffs. He was named the 1959 NBA Rookie-of-the-Year. He appeared in 11 NBA All-Star games and was named game co-MVP in 1959. He holds the NBA All-Star game record for most career free throws attempted (98) and made (78).

To cap off a wonderful basketball career, Elgin was named to the NBA 35th Anniversary All-Time Team and enshrined at the Basketball Hall of Fame.

Top: *One of the best one-on-one players ever, Elgin Baylor began his drives with a rocking motion.*

Right: *Grace and the unique ability to hang in the air marked Baylor's game.*

Opposite: *At his best in the playoffs, Elgin scored 3623 points – fourth on the all-time list.*

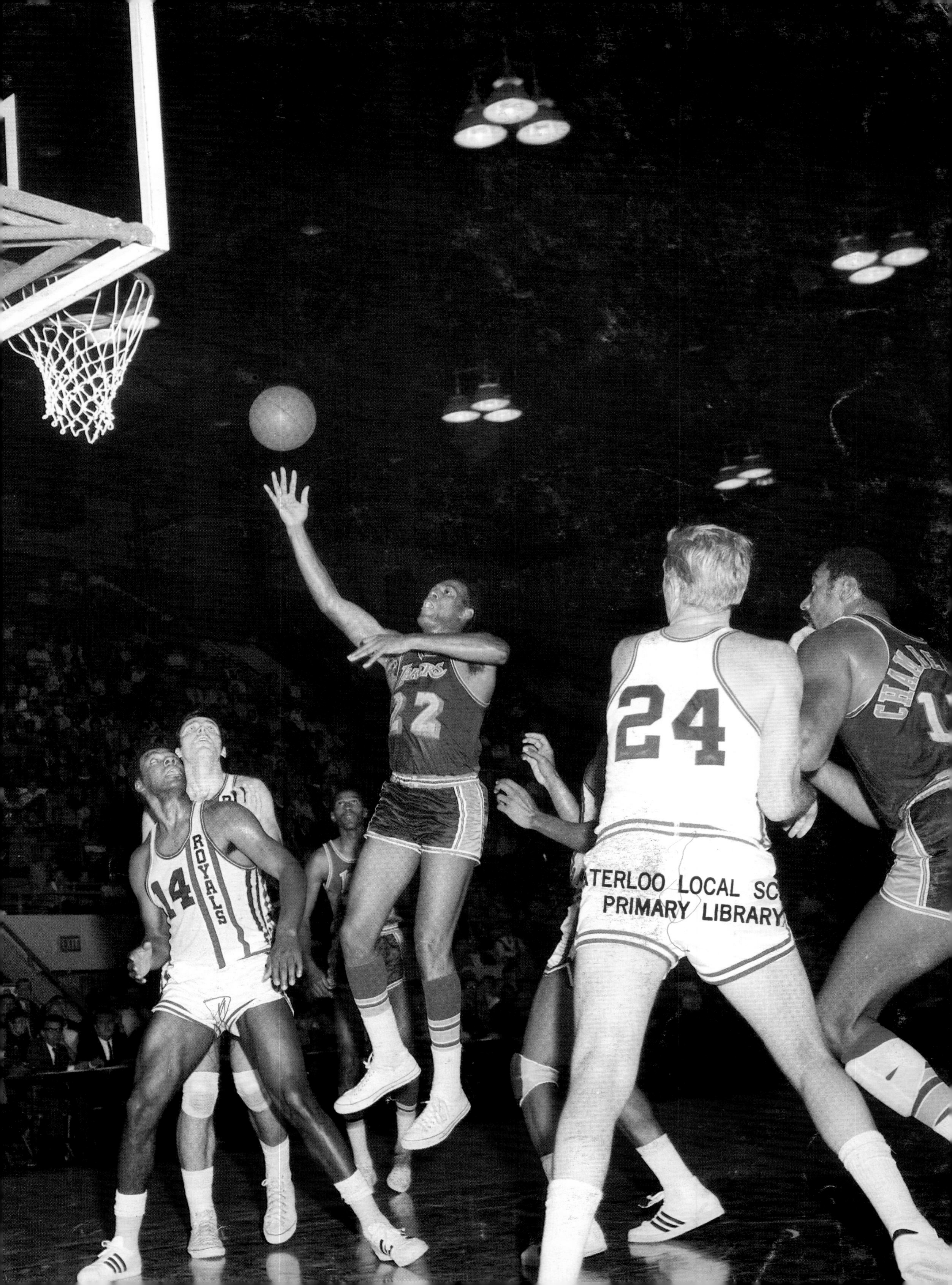
22
ROYALS
14
24

Johnny Beckman

Johnny Beckman began his remarkable 17-year career in New York's West Side, near his birthplace, as a member of St. Gabriel's in 1910. As a great established professional, he played with the Hudson County Opals, West Hoboken, and Troys of Union Hill in the Interstate, New York State, New England, and Eastern leagues.

In 1922, 'Becky' became captain of the Original Celtics and became basketball's biggest box office attraction of the era. This Hall of Famer was called 'The Babe Ruth of Basketball,' and was considered 'The History Maker of the Century in Basketball.' The Baltimore Orioles (a basketball team of that era) acquired him in 1927 for the unprecedented figure of $10,000. He was elected to the all-time pro teams in polls in 1930, 1946, and 1950. In 1935 Beckman was selected as Basketball's Finest Competitive Athlete.

Right: *Johnny Beckman of the Original Celtics with baseball superstar Babe Ruth.*

Opposite: *In 12 pro seasons Dave Bing averaged 20.3 points per game and led the NBA in scoring in 1968.*

Bottom: *Walt Bellamy was NBA Rookie-of-the-Year in 1962 with a 31.6 scoring average.*

Walt Bellamy

Walt Bellamy was a two-time All-American at Indiana University, where he averaged 20.6 points per game. He was a member of the 1960 gold medal U.S. Olympic team and is enshrined at the U.S. Olympic Hall of Fame. The Chicago Packers of the NBA drafted him in the first round of the 1961 draft.

In his first year, Bellamy was named NBA Rookie-of-the-Year as he averaged 31.6 points per game and led the league in field goal percentage. His 31.6 points was the second-best average ever by a rookie. Bellamy, who was very consistent but only made it to the Championship series once, played 13 seasons with six different teams. The 6ft 11in center scored 20,941 points (ninth on the all-time list) with an average of 20.1 points per game and 14,241 rebounds (sixth on the all-time list). 'Big Bell' played in four NBA All-Star games, and was the seventh player in NBA history to score 20,000 points. Though an excellent center, he was overshadowed by two other great centers of that era: Bill Russell and Wilt Chamberlain.

Dave Bing

Known as a slashing and smooth player, Dave Bing was the number one pick of the 1966 draft by the Detroit Pistons. The two-time All-American at Syracuse University had averaged 24.8 points per game and was possibly the greatest guard in Syracuse history. He went on to play 12 NBA seasons. He was named the 1967 NBA Rookie-of-the-Year; named to the All-NBA First Team twice; named to the All-NBA Second Team once; and led the league in scoring with an average of 27.1 points per game.

A 6ft 3in guard, he averaged 20.3 points per game during his professional career and scored 18,327 career points to place him 22nd on the all-time list. He played in seven NBA All-Star games and was named the game MVP in 1976. A good scorer, Bing gave Detroit and their fans alot of memories but, despite his fine performance, could not bring home a World Championship for the franchise.

Larry Bird

The best all-around player in the game today, Larry Bird can do it all. He is the master of fundamentals. Through nine seasons, all with Boston, he has developed into one of the greatest players ever to play the sport of basketball. During his career, he has been named the 1980 NBA Rookie-of-the-Year, named to the All-NBA First Team for nine consecutive years, named to the All-NBA Defensive Team three times, and named the league's Most Valuable Player for three consecutive years.

The Boston Celtics drafted him in the 1978 draft as a junior eligible in the first round, but he chose to play his senior year. In three years of basketball at Indiana State University, the two-time All-American averaged 30.3 points per game. The 1979 College Player-of-the-Year singlehandedly turned Indiana State into a national powerhouse as it was runner-up to Michigan State and 'Magic' Johnson in the 1979 NCAA Finals.

The 6 ft 9 in forward has a career average of 25 points per game, which places him 26th on the all-time NBA scorers' list with 17,783 points. He led the league in free throw percentage three times and is currently fourth in the all-time career free throw percentage category. He has played in nine NBA All-Star games and was the game MVP in 1982. Bird has led the Celtics to three Championship titles. He was named the 1984 and 1986 Playoff MVP. In 145 playoff games, he has averaged 24.5 points per game and holds the NBA playoff record for most points in one year (632 in 1984). He is also the NBA's all-time three-point field goal leader with 455. Bird is one of the best players in the history of basketball, as his statistics and awards show.

Above: *Larry Bird, an All-NBA First Team pick for nine straight years.*

Right: *Bird's jumper makes him the all-time three-point field goal leader.*

Opposite: *Deadly at the foul line, Bird has led the NBA in free throw percentage three times.*

Benny Borgmann

Upon completing a brilliant high school career in Clifton, New Jersey in 1917, Bernhard 'Benny' Borgmann toured the country in a career that included 2500 professional games. He was recognized as an All-Time All-Pro, playing in the American, National, Metropolitan, Eastern, New York State, and Western Massachusetts leagues. This 5 ft 8 in Hall of Famer was always one of the highest scorers, frequently scoring ten or more points when his team totaled only 20. Borgmann was in demand by many teams and cities wherever professional ball was played.

Right: *Benny Borgmann, at 5 ft 8 in, played in 2500 pro games.*

Bill Bradley

On 30 December 1964, one of the greatest individual performances in college basketball history was turned in by Princeton University's Bill Bradley. He single-handedly almost beat Michigan, the number one team in the nation. With 4:37 left on the clock, Bradley fouled out after having scored 41 points to put his team up by 12 (75-63). Without him on the floor, his team fell apart and eventually lost 80-78. Hall of Famer Joe Lapchick called Bradley's performance the greatest he had ever seen.

Bradley averaged 30.2 points per game during his college career and was a two-time All-American. He was named the College Player-of-the-Year in 1964 and 1965 and was the first basketball player to win the Amateur Athletic Union (AAU) Sullivan Award as the nation's most outstanding athlete. He captained the 1964 U.S. Olympic team in Tokyo to a gold medal. In

1965, Bradley led Princeton to the NCAA Final Four and finished in third place, an incredible feat considering that the Ivy League is geared more towards academics than athletics.

Drafted in the first round by the New York Knicks, Bradley played ten seasons in the NBA after taking time out to attend Oxford University. During his professional career, he scored 9217 points and had 2533 assists. He played on two World Championship teams with the Knicks, in 1970 and 1973. Day in and day out, 'Dollar Bill' was one of the more steady and consistent players in the league. He was an outstanding team player and leader who seemed constantly in motion.

In 1978 he became a U.S. Senator for New Jersey. His basketball career was honored in 1982 when he was enshrined at the Basketball Hall of Fame.

Al Cervi

Al Cervi was regarded as a great scorer and defensive player, a fine clutch performer, and one of his era's greatest professional competitors. At the age of 20, he began playing pro ball in 1938 for the Buffalo Bisons of the National Basketball League. He immediately made an impact as he was selected the NBL's MVP. At that point his professional career was interrupted while he served five years during World War II.

Upon returning to the NBL, Cervi joined the Rochester Royals and was selected All-Pro as he led Rochester to the 1945 NBL Championship. The following season the Royals repeated as World Champs as he led the league in scoring, was named MVP, and was selected All-Pro. The Syracuse Nationals hired him as a player-coach and he led them to the 1949 Championship. Cervi was selected All-Pro and was named the NBL's Coach-of-the-Year. As the team merged with the NBA for the 1950 season, he was selected All-NBA Second Team and was named Coach-of-the-Year. He finally retired in 1953. This Hall of Famer was selected by the *Sporting News* in 1962 as one of the best backcourt players of his time.

Above: *In 1946 Al Cervi led the NBL in scoring and was named MVP.*

Left: *Bill Bradley scored 30.2 points per game during his Princeton days. As a pro, his motion game and pin-point shooting helped the Knicks to two NBA titles.*

Wilt Chamberlain

Top left and above: *Inside Wilt was awesome, scoring 31,419 career points – the second best in NBA history.*

Top right and opposite: *Wilt the Stilt is the only player ever to score over 4000 points in one season.*

The question in basketball that everybody asks – 'Who is the greatest player in the game – Wilt Chamberlain, Bill Russell, or Kareem Abdul-Jabbar?' – may be resolved by consulting the NBA record book. When Wilt Chamberlain ended his 14-year career in 1973, he held or shared 43 NBA records. He scored 100 points in a single game. (The closest anyone has come to this is scoring 73 points.) He averaged 50.4 points a game for one season. He was the first and only player to score over 4000 points in a season and the first to score 30,000 points in a career. He scored 50 or more points in a game 118 times and 40 or more in 271 games. He is the only player to have a career scoring average of over 30 points per game. Wilt is the second leading scorer in NBA history with 31,419 (behind Kareem) and is the all-time leading rebounder with 23,924. He holds the record for most rebounds in a game with 55.

The 7 ft 1 in center played two seasons at the University of Kansas where he averaged 29.9 points per game and 18.3 rebounds. He led the team to the NCAA Finals in 1957 where the Jayhawks lost a memorable game in triple overtime to North Carolina. Even though he still had one year of eligibility left at Kansas, he decided to leave school. He joined the magicians of basketball – the Harlem Globetrotters – for one season to broaden his basketball skills.

'Wilt the Stilt' was drafted by the Philadelphia Warriors in 1959 in the first round. He was named NBA Rookie-of-the-Year and MVP of the NBA All-Star game in 1960. He went on to appear in 13 NBA All-Star games. Wilt led his teams to 13 playoff appearances and came away with two Championships. He was

named Playoff MVP in 1972 and the NBA's MVP four times (three consecutive years). He led the league in scoring seven straight times, rebounding 11 times, and field goal percentage nine times. He even led the league in assists in 1968 after he was criticized for not passing the ball. In 1218 games (over 55,800 minutes) including regular-season, playoff, and All-Star games, Wilt Chamberlain never fouled out. He is third on the all-time list for minutes played.

Chamberlain's great basketball career ended with his election to the NBA 35th Anniversary All-Time Team and into the Basketball Hall of Fame. Surely 'The Big Dipper' deserves to be called the greatest basketball player of all time.

Opposite: *Wilt's fingertip roll was a classic and unstoppable.*

Right: *Upon retirement in 1973, Wilt held or shared 43 NBA records including most points in a game (100) and most rebounds in a game (55).*

Charles Cooper

After graduating in 1925 from Central High School in Philadelphia, Pennsylvania, Charles Cooper began his 20-year professional career with the Philadelphia Panther Pros and continued from 1926 to 1929 with the Philadelphia Giants. This Hall of Famer then joined the New York Renaissance for 11 brilliant years, during which the Rens won 1303 and lost only 203. In 1932-33

the Rens won 88 straight games.

At 6 ft 4 in, 'Tarzan' was a superb center and was considered the team MVP as the leader of the Rens squad that won the World Professional Championship in 1939. Acclaimed the greatest center of his era, Cooper later led the Washington Bears to the World Professional title in 1943.

Left: *Charles Cooper (second from right) was recognized as the greatest center of his era.*

Bob Cousy

Known as 'Mr. Basketball,' Bob Cousy was one of the most popular players in the history of the game and lifted the pro game to major status. He was the best playmaker and floor leader in the game. Cousy was the most electrifying player of his time and set the tone for the point guards of today.

For 17 years – four with Holy Cross, 13 with Boston – Cousy dazzled the fans of New England with his unique style of play. At Holy Cross he was an All-American and led them to an NCAA Division I Championship. Cousy was drafted in the first round by Tri-Cities in 1950, but before playing in any games he was traded to Chicago and then picked up in the dispersal draft by the Celtics.

He became their leader as soon as he stepped onto the court. The 6ft 1in point guard 'quarterbacked' the Boston Celtics to six NBA Championships. He played in 13 NBA All-Star games – in fact the first 13 games ever, a feat no other player duplicated – and was named game MVP in 1954 and 1957. With his passing talents, he led the league in assists for eight straight years – a record for the most seasons in leading the league. He is fourth on the all-time list for most career assists with 6955, and second on the list for most assists in one game with 28.

No one had ever passed the way Cousy did – by looking one way while sending the ball in another direction. He was the innovator of the passing game. There have been few players as clever and intelligent as Bob Cousy. He would attempt the most intricate shots or passes in the most tense moments of the game. He was a clutch player and just by being on the floor, he would inspire the team. At a time before the 24-second clock, Cousy would dribble the ball all over the court until the clock ran out, with the opposing players frantically chasing him to try to catch up with him but with no success.

To conclude a remarkable basketball career, 'Mr. Basketball' was elected to the Basketball Hall of Fame and was named to the NBA 35th Anniversary All-Time Team. He retired in 1963, and will be remembered as one of the most exciting players in the game.

Left: *Bob Cousy's quick hands controlled the ball in traffic and put him fourth in career assists. He made a career of scooting by his defender and whipping passes to open teammates.*

Opposite: *Although only 6ft 1in, Cousy could drive the lane. A natural leader, he led the Celtics to six NBA Championships.*

Dave Cowens

Dave Cowens was 'a big man who thought big and played big.' He was comparatively small for a center but he made up for his physical size by an aggressive desire to win, an ability to shoot a deadly accurate jump shot, and a complete mastery of the fundamentals of play as a center.

The 6ft 8in red-headed center from Florida State University was drafted fourth by the Boston Celtics in 1970. In ten seasons, he led them to two NBA World Championships. He appeared in seven NBA All-Star games and was named game MVP in 1973.

During his career, he was awarded NBA co-Rookie-of-the-Year honors in 1971 and was the NBA's MVP in 1973 with averages of 20.5 points and 14.9 rebounds per game. In 1976, he was named to the All-NBA Defensive First Team and was named player-coach for the 1978-79 season. After retiring in 1980, he tried a comeback with Milwaukee for the 1982-83 season.

Dave was known for giving it his all in every game, as he did in the 1974 NBA Final when he knocked the ball out of an offensive player's hands, chased it, and then dove fully extended to keep the ball from going out of bounds. Cowens must have slid nearly ten feet, exemplifying his desire to win.

Opposite and above: *Dave Cowens of the Boston Celtics.*

Billy Cunningham

At the University of North Carolina, Billy Cunningham, a two-time All-American, averaged 24.8 points per game and was an Academic All-American as well. The Philadelphia 76ers drafted him in the first round of the 1965 draft. Cunningham played 11 years of professional basketball, nine in the NBA and two in the ABA. In his nine-year NBA career with Philadelphia, this Hall of Famer was named to the All-NBA Rookie Team, the All-NBA First Team three times, the All-NBA Second Team once, and played in four NBA All-Star games. He averaged 20.8 points per game and was a member of the 76ers' 1967 Championship team. A fierce, all-around competitor, he was known best for his jumping ability.

After the 1972 season, the 6ft 7in forward jumped to the American Basketball Association (ABA) to play for the Carolina Cougars. During this two-year stint, he was named the 1973 ABA MVP, led the league in steals, played in one ABA All-Star game, and was named to the 1973 All-ABA First Team. 'The Kangaroo Kid' returned to the NBA for his final two years of professional basketball.

Left: *A leaper, Billy Cunningham made the All-NBA First Team three times.*

Bob Dandridge

Bob Dandridge averaged 22.6 points per game during his college career at Norfolk State University. He was drafted by the Milwaukee Bucks in the fourth round of the 1969 draft as he began a 13-year professional career (nine with Milwaukee and four with Washington). Dandridge, a complete player, made the 1970 All-NBA Rookie Team, was named to the 1979 All-NBA Second Team and to the 1979 All-NBA Defensive First Team, and played in four NBA All-Star games.

At 6 ft 6 in, he had a career average of 18.5 points per game and 20.1 points per game during the playoffs. He was a member of the Milwaukee Bucks' 1971 World Championship team and the Washington Bullets' 1978 World Championship team. He is one of only a few players to have played in two World Championships with two different teams. Dandridge was a good scorer and was known for his defensive play. He retired in 1982.

Adrian Dantley

A 13-year NBA veteran, Adrian Dantley will be remembered as a scorer. He averaged 30 points per game for four straight years. This NBA journeyman has played for six different teams and averaged 25.5 points per game with 21,058 career points, which places him 11th on the all-time scoring list. The only teams he has played on that had championship potential are his last two teams, the Detroit Pistons and the Dallas Mavericks.

The Buffalo Braves drafted him with their first pick as a hardship case in 1976 out of the University of Notre Dame. The 6 ft 5 in two-time All-American averaged 25.8 points per game in three years. Dantley was a member of the 1976 gold medal U.S. Olympic team. He was named the 1977 NBA Rookie-of-the-Year, named to the All-NBA Second Team twice, led the league in scoring twice, and was the 1984 NBA Comeback Player-of-the-Year. He has played in six NBA All-Star games. Dantley shares an NBA record for most free throws made in one game, with 28.

Opposite: *Bob Dandridge's quickness enabled him to score and defend.*

This page: *Strong inside moves have made Adrian Dantley a top scorer.*

Bob Davies

Bob Davies is recognized as one of the great 'little men' who have played the game of basketball. He was considered the pioneer of playmaking before the Bob Cousy era. 'The Blond Bomber' pleased the crowd with his flashy passes and his original behind-the-back dribble.

At Seton Hall he turned the school into a national power. Between 1939 and 1941, he led the Pirates to 43 consecutive wins by averaging 11.2 points per game. After graduation, he enlisted in the military but was still able to play in the American Basketball League.

Upon the completion of his military duty, the 6ft 1in point guard was signed as a free agent by the Rochester Royals in 1945 to play in the National Basketball League. During his three years in the NBL, he participated in two All-Star games, was named league MVP, and led the Royals to a Championship. When the NBL merged into the NBA, Davies continued for seven more years with the Royals. He participated in four NBA All-Star games, led the league in assists, and was a member of the Royals' Championship team in 1951. This Hall of Famer was named to the NBA 25th Anniversary All-Time Team in 1970.

Dave DeBusschere

Dave DeBusschere may have been the least recognized basketball star of all time. It was not until he was traded to the New York Knicks in 1968 that he began to be recognized for his playing abilities. He quickly became basketball's newest overnight sensation.

At the University of Detroit, he was the hometown hero and was named All-American for three years. In 1960, he was named the Michigan Amateur Athlete-of-the-Year.

Dave was a talented baseball pitcher as well. At the start, he was undecided in which direction to go, so he played both professional basketball and baseball. He signed with the Chicago White Sox and was drafted on the first round by the Detroit Pistons in 1962. He played both sports until Detroit asked him to become player-coach at the age of 24, the youngest in NBA history. After two-and-a-half years, he gave up coaching and concentrated solely on playing basketball.

Upon being traded to the Knicks, the 6ft 6in forward played an integral part in their only World Championships (1970 and 1973). He was named to the All-NBA Defensive First Team for six straight years (1969-74) and played in eight NBA All-Star games. Dave holds the record for the most field goals in one quarter of an All-Star game, with eight. During his career, he scored 14,053 points and pulled down 9618 rebounds. He was one of the best all-around forwards who has ever played the game. The Hall of Famer was a good perimeter shooter, had inside strength, rebounding power, excellent defense, and had the instincts for doing the right thing at the right time.

Opposite: *Bob Davies showed his playmaking skills in four NBA All-Star games.*

Right: *Dave DeBusschere played excellent defense and hit the outside shot.*

Dutch Dehnert

Without high school or collegiate training, Henry Dehnert began his memorable basketball career playing in the Eastern Pennsylvania State, New York State, and New England leagues before joining the Original Celtics in 1920. To make an easy game interesting while the Celtics were dominating eastern basketball for eight years, 'Dutch' went to the foul line to receive passes from his famous Celtics teammates. The pivot play was born, and this Hall of Famer became famous for its execution and success.

At 6 ft 1 in, he played with the Cleveland Rosenblums and won American League titles in 1928, 1929, and 1930. Dehnert coached the Detroit Eagles to world titles in 1940 and 1941, and the Sheboygan (Wisconsin) Redskins to western titles in 1945 and 1946. Though he invented the pivot play by chance, he played and coached it so well that the three-second rule was adopted.

Right: *Henry 'Dutch' Dehnert, who invented the pivot play while with the Original Celtics in the early and mid 1920s.*

Paul Endacott

Paul Endacott was graduated from Lawrence High School in 1919 and the University of Kansas in 1923. After being selected as an All-State guard in 1919, Endacott became the 'Greatest Player Ever Coached' by Kansas' fabled 'Phog' Allen. He was selected All-Conference Second Team in 1921 and First Team in 1922 and 1923. At 6 ft 0 in, he led the Jayhawks to a mythical national title in 1923 which included the first-ever undefeated conference season. 'Endy' was selected by the Helms Foundation as National Player-of-the-Year in 1923 and was honored as the All-Time Kansas Player in 1924 by the inventor of the game of basketball, Dr. James Naismith.

In 1943, he was selected to the Helms All-Time All-American Second Team. Endacott was chosen by Dr. Allen in 1951 as a member of the National All-Time College Team. This Hall of Famer was the recipient of the 1969 Sportsmen's World Award in basketball as 'an athlete whose championship performances have stood the test of time and whose exemplary personal conduct has made him an outstanding inspiration for youth to emulate.'

Right: *Alex English shoots his jumper over two defenders.*

Alex English

Alex English's professional career began very slowly. In two years with the Milwaukee Bucks, he averaged 7.7 points per game. English has since developed into one of the NBA's most consistent scorers. He led the league in scoring with an average of 28.4 points per game in 1983. The Milwaukee Bucks drafted him in the second round of the 1976 draft out of the University of South Carolina, where he had averaged 17.8 points per game.

In 12 seasons he has played for the Milwaukee Bucks, the Indiana Pacers, and the Denver Nuggets. The 6 ft 7 in forward has scored 21,242 career points, placing him tenth on the all-time scoring list. He has been named to the All-NBA Second Team three times and has played in seven NBA All-Star games. He has seen his most productive seasons with his current team, the Denver Nuggets. He is currently seventh in most field goals made and ninth in field goals attempted. English is one of 14 players ever to score over 20,000 career points.

Julius Erving

Julius Erving was the flashiest player ever to play the game. His acrobatic style set the precedent for the players of today. He helped popularize the sport of basketball as the fans came out just to see his magic.

While at the University of Massachusetts, Erving averaged 26.3 points and 20.1 rebounds per game. He was one of only seven players to average over 20 points and 20 rebounds per game during his NCAA career. The Virginia Squires of the American Basketball Association (ABA) signed him as an undergraduate free agent in 1971. He played two seasons there and was named to the All-ABA Rookie Team. In 1973, Erving was traded to the ABA's New York Nets. In three seasons with the Nets, he was named the 1975 ABA co-MVP, the 1974 and 1976 ABA MVP, and the 1974 and 1976 ABA Playoff MVP. He was also named to the All-ABA Defensive Team, and was a member of the 1974 and 1976 ABA Championship teams. At 6 ft 7 in, he led the league in scoring for three years, was named to the All-ABA First Team for four consecutive years, played in five consecutive NBA All-Star games, averaged 31.1 points in 48 playoff games, and finished his ABA career with the highest career scoring average at 28.7 points per game.

When the ABA folded and the Nets merged with the NBA in 1976, Erving was sold to the Philadelphia

76ers. He went on to an 11-year career and was named to the All-NBA First Team five times, played in ten consecutive NBA All-Star games, was named the MVP of the 1977 and 1983 NBA All-Star games, named the 1981 League MVP, and was a member of the 76ers' 1983 World Championship team.

In his 16-year ABA/NBA career, 'Dr. J' scored 30,026 career points. Erving is one of three players ever to score over 30,000 points. His combined stats would place him third in points scored and first in steals, although the NBA only recognizes NBA stats.

Left: *'Dr J.' stuffs. Only two other players have also scored over 30,000 career points.*

Top: *Julius Erving electrified crowds with his swooping drives to the basket.*

Patrick Ewing

Left: *An intimidator on defense, Patrick Ewing was College Player-of-the-Year in 1985 and was drafted by the New York Knicks as the number one pick.*

Opposite: *Bevo Francis of Rio Grande College scored 113 points in one game – a collegiate record.*

Patrick Ewing will go down in history as one of the most dominant players ever to play college basketball. During his four years, Georgetown University reached the NCAA Final three times and won the 1984 Championship. The three-time All-American led the Hoyas to a 121-23 record. He was named the 1984 NCAA Division I Tournament Most Outstanding Player and the 1985 College Player-of-the-Year.

The New York Knicks drafted him as the number one pick of the 1985 draft. The 7ft 0in center was named the 1986 NBA Rookie-of-the-Year, named to the All-NBA Second Team once, named to the All-NBA Defensive Second Team once, and selected to play in two NBA All-Star games. In his first three seasons as a professional, all with the Knicks, he averaged 20.5 points per game.

Bevo Francis

Bevo Francis exploded onto the college scene in 1953-54. He attended Rio Grande College in Ohio, which had an enrollment of only 92 students. Rio Grande went 39-0 in his freshman year and 21-7 in his sophomore year.

Bevo was the 'most publicized and most prolific record-breaking basketball player in the game.' The 6 ft 9 in center was a scoring machine. He holds many NCAA Division II records: most points scored in a game (113), the highest season scoring average (46.5 points per game), most field goals in a game (38), most free throws made in a game (37), and most free throws attempted in a season (510). A basketball phenomenon, Bevo totaled 1176 field goals, 898 free throws, 3250 career points, and a career average of 50.1 for only two seasons. He led Rio Grande from the Rio Grande Gym (capacity 150) to Madison Square Garden (the hotbed of college hoops with a capacity of 13,000). Bevo Francis quit college to turn professional and toured with the Boston Whirlwinds, opponents of the Harlem Globetrotters. He retired in 1964, without fulfilling his dream of playing in the NBA.

Walt Frazier

In ten seasons with the New York Knicks, Walt Frazier was known as a defensive specialist. He was selected to the All-NBA Defensive First Team seven times during his career.

'Clyde the Glide' was a surprise first round draft choice (fifth overall) in 1967 by the Knicks out of Southern Illinois University, a Division II college. His attitude fit New York perfectly. He was known for being suave, arrogant, and proud. New York considered Walt Frazier a real-life hero. He thrived on the hometown crowd. He had nerves of steel and was a clutch player. The Hall of Famer scored 15,581 points during his 13-year career. He played in seven NBA All-Star games and was named MVP of the game in 1975. He led New York to two World Championships in 1970 and 1973.

'Clyde' will be forever remembered not only for his on-court accomplishments, but also for all the publicity he brought to the NBA with his savvy and flamboyant lifestyle.

Left: *Walt Frazier was smooth on and off the court.*

Below: *His lightning-quick hands made him a defensive star and floor leader.*

Max Friedman

Max Friedman was graduated in 1908 from the Hebrew Tech Institute in New York City. He played with the 1906-08 University Settlement House Metropolitan AAU Champions before turning professional with the New York Roosevelts in 1909. Friedman played in every professional league in the East. He was acknowledged as one of the great defensive stars and the leader of each team for which he played, including Newburgh, 1911-12; Hudson, 1913, in the Hudson River League; Utica, 1914, in the New York State League; Carbondale, 1915, in the Pennsylvania League; the Philadelphia Jaspers, 1916-17 in the Eastern League; Albany, 1920, in the New York State League; and Easthampton, Massachusetts, 1921-22, in the Interstate League.

'Marty' finished his extraordinary career as captain and coach of the Cleveland Rosenblums from 1923 through 1927. This Hall of Famer won championships with nearly all of his teams. He won 35 straight games with Carbondale in 1915 and won the American League Championship with the Salukis in 1926 and 1927. Friedman captained the AEF champions, the Tours Team, who won the 1919 Inter-Allied Games. He also played brilliantly with the independent New York Whirlwinds. At 5 ft 8 in, Friedman and his pal, Barney Sedran, were called the 'Heavenly Twins.'

Right: *Hall of Famer Max Friedman was a leader and defensive star who took most of his teams to championships in the 1910s and 1920s.*

Joe Fulks

Joe Fulks was the first super-scorer of the modern era of professional basketball. In 1947 as a 27-year-old rookie, he led the Basketball Association of America (BAA) in scoring with an average of 23.2 points per game, an amazing feat in his era, comparable to averaging 46 points a game today. To show what an oddity this was, the runner-up in scoring in 1947 averaged 16.7 points per game.

The 6 ft 5 in guard attended Murray State College but left to join the military. He was signed by the Philadelphia Warriors after completing his tour of duty in 1946. He is considered the first superstar of the BAA and NBA. Joe was a scoring machine and finished his career with a 16.4 scoring average. During his eight-year career, all with the Warriors, he was named to the All-NBA First Team three times, led the NBA in free throw percentage, played in two NBA All-Star games, and was a member of the 1947 NBA Championship team. He holds the record for the second-best performance for a rookie in an NBA Championship series with 37 points. Any scoring record set in the late 1940s that still holds today is amazing. In Joe Fulks' time there was no 24-second clock, so the game was nowhere near as fast-paced as today's game, making his record all the more remarkable.

'Jumping Joe' helped revolutionize the jump shot, and this Hall of Famer will always be remembered for his scoring capabilities.

Laddie Gale

Lauren 'Laddie' Gale was graduated from Oakridge High School in 1935 and the University of Oregon in 1939. In 1935, he was an Oregon All-State selection as a four-year regular in high school. As a college junior and senior, he scored a total of 815 points and led the University of Oregon to the Pacific Coast title and the first NCAA Tournament Championship in 1939. He was selected to the All-Pacific Coast Conference First Team in 1938 and 1939. At 6 ft 5 in, he led the conference in scoring both years and was All-American in 1939.

Gale played professional basketball with the Detroit Eagles and Salt Lake City Desert Times. He was selected to the All-Time Pacific Coast Northern Division Team and to the Oregon Hall of Fame in 1964, the first year he was eligible. This Hall of Famer was a star player of the 'Tall Firs,' who brought national recognition to Pacific Northwest basketball.

Left: *Laddie Gale led Oregon to the first NCAA Tournament Championship in 1939.*

Opposite: *An offensive star, Joe Fulks scored heavily with his jump shot.*

George Gervin

At Eastern Michigan University, George Gervin averaged 26.8 points per game in two seasons. The Virginia Squires of the American Basketball Association (ABA) selected him as an undergraduate in the first round of the 1973 ABA draft. In four ABA seasons with Virginia and San Antonio, he played in three ABA All-Star games and was named to the All-ABA Second Team twice.

'The Iceman' entered the NBA in 1976 with San Antonio during the ABA/NBA merger. In ten NBA seasons (1977-86), he was one of the most prolific scorers in NBA history with 20,708 points and an average of 26.2 points per game. His 20,708 points places him 14th on the all-time scoring list, and he has the fifth-best career average. He is one of 14 players to score over 20,000 career points. He was named to the All-NBA First Team five times and the All-NBA Second Team twice. Gervin played in nine NBA All-Star games and was named game MVP in 1980, when he scored 34 points. The 6 ft 7 in guard led the league in scoring for four years (making him one of two players in NBA history to win four scoring titles) and holds the NBA record for most points in a quarter with 33. Gervin was known as a great scorer, but he never played on a championship team.

Below left: *George Gervin had extraordinary firepower and the ability to shoot off-balance.*

Below: *Gervin's deadly jumper got him a career average of 26.2 points per game – fifth best ever.*

Artis Gilmore

At Jacksonville University, Artis Gilmore averaged 24.3 points and 22.7 rebounds per game. He is one of seven players to average over 20 points and 20 rebounds per game during his college career. In 1970, the two-time All-American led Jacksonville to the NCAA Final Four, where they lost to UCLA in the Championship game. He was named to the All-NCAA Final Four Tournament Team. He led the NCAA in rebounding in 1970 and 1971 and is the NCAA career leader in rebounding with an average of 22.7.

The Kentucky Colonels drafted him in the first round of the 1971 American Basketball Association (ABA) draft. During his five years in the ABA, he was named the 1972 ABA Rookie-of-the-Year and the ABA MVP, named to the All-ABA First Team five times, named to the All-ABA Defensive Team four times, led the ABA in rebounding four times, led the league in field goal percentage twice, and led the ABA in blocked

shots once. Gilmore played in five ABA All-Star games and was named the 1974 game MVP. The Colonels won the 1975 ABA Championship, and Gilmore was named the Playoff MVP.

The Chicago Bulls selected him in the dispersal draft when the ABA merged with the NBA. In 12 seasons, with three different teams, Gilmore has averaged 17.1 points per game. The 7 ft 2 in center is the NBA all-time field goal percentage leader. He has led the league in field goal percentage four times, been named to the All-NBA Defensive Second Team once, and played in six NBA All-Star games. Gilmore was known as a great rebounder with a soft shooting touch.

Top: *Tough under the boards, Artis Gilmore is also the NBA's all-time field goal percentage leader.*

Tom Gola

Tom Gola led La Salle College to a 92-76 win over Bradley to capture the 1954 NCAA Tournament Championship. The MVP of that tournament, Gola captured many hearts as one of the greatest collegiate players ever to step onto the hardwood.

He was considered one of the greatest high school players to come out of the city of Philadelphia by scoring 2222 points. Tom went on to his college career at La Salle and accomplished everything there was to accomplish. He was named All-American all four years and helped win the National Invitational Tournament (NIT) Championship in 1952 and the NCAA Championship in 1954, one of only a few players who have won both championships during their careers. He is one of two players to score over 2000 points and grab over 2000 rebounds in college.

The 6 ft 6 in forward was selected in the 1955 draft by the Philadelphia Warriors on the first round. He played ten seasons with three teams but enjoyed his greatest success in Philadelphia. In 1956, he was a member of the Warriors' NBA Championship team. Throughout his professional career he was selected to play in five NBA All-Star games. Over his career, he averaged 11.3 points per game. This Hall of Famer was a steady professional but will go down in basketball history as one of the greatest collegiate players.

Left: *In the 1950s Tom Gola was a four-time All-American at La Salle and scored over 2000 points. As a pro, he played in five All-Star games and was known for helping young players with their games.*

Opposite: *A sharpshooting left-hander, Gail Goodrich averaged 18.6 points per game over 14 NBA seasons. His quick shot and up-tempo game were keys to UCLA's national titles in 1964 and 1965.*

Gail Goodrich

Gail Goodrich averaged 19 points per game during his college career at UCLA. The All-American was a member of the 1964 and 1965 NCAA Division I Championship team.

The Los Angeles Lakers drafted Goodrich in the first round of the 1965 draft. He enjoyed a 14-year professional career (1966-79) with three different teams and scored a career 19,181 points (17th on the all-time career scoring list). Over his illustrious career, he averaged 18.6 points per game with a best season average of 25.9 points per game in 1972. The 6 ft 1 in guard was named to the 1974 All-NBA First Team and played in five NBA All-Star games. With the Lakers, he reached the NBA World Championship four times, winning the title in 1972. In 80 playoff games, he averaged 18.1 points per game. Goodrich was a very smooth, consistent left-hander with an excellent outside shot.

Hal Greer

Hal Greer was a durable and reliable player. In 1958, he was drafted by the Syracuse Nationals out of Marshall College where he averaged 19.4 points and 10.7 rebounds per game. Of his 15 NBA seasons with the Nats and Philadelphia 76ers (same franchise), his teams made the playoffs 13 times. He averaged 27.7 points during the 1967 playoffs, and won an NBA Championship with the 76ers in 1967. Over his 15-year professional career, he played in ten NBA All-Star games and was named the MVP of the 1968 game, as he scored a record 19 points in one quarter.

The 6ft 2in guard scored a regular-season total of 21,586 points for a career average of 19.2. Hal is ninth on the list of NBA career scorers. He is fifth on the NBA list for most games played (1122); seventh for most minutes played (39,788); ninth for most field goals made (8504); and eighth for most field goals attempted (18,811). The team's all-time leading scorer, the Philadelphia 76ers honored this Hall of Famer by retiring his number 15.

Cliff Hagan

Right: *Cliff Hagan's soft hook shot and steady play helped the St. Louis Hawks win five NBA Championships.*

Opposite: *Hal Greer drives sharply to the basket. Greer is ninth among NBA career scorers.*

At the University of Kentucky, Cliff Hagan played four seasons of college basketball in five years (Kentucky did not have a team in 1952-53). The two-time All-American averaged 19.2 points per game and was a member of the 1951 NCAA Championship team.

Before completing a two-year military service, Boston picked him in the third round of the 1953 draft. Hagan and Ed Macauley were traded to St. Louis in exchange for Bill Russell in 1956. In 12 professional seasons, Hagan played ten years with St. Louis (1957-66) and two with the Dallas Chapperals of the ABA (1968

and 1969). He averaged 18 points per game during his NBA career. The 6 ft 4 in forward led St. Louis to six Western Division Championships, four NBA World Championship appearances, and the 1958 NBA title. In the playoffs, the Hall of Famer averaged 20.4 points per game. He was named to the 1958 and 1959 All-NBA Second Team and was chosen to play in five NBA All-Star games.

The Dallas Chapperals signed Hagan in 1967 as a player-coach, where he averaged 15.1 points per game and played in the 1968 ABA All-Star game.

John Havlicek

John Havlicek was an outstanding athlete and while in high school was named All-Ohio for three different sports. His success continued at Ohio State University, where he scored 1223 points and helped the Buckeyes to one NCAA title in 1960 and two runner-up positions as the team won 78 and lost 6 in his three years. The Boston Celtics drafted him as their number one pick in the first round but the Cleveland Browns of the NFL also drafted him in the seventh round as a wide receiver. He attempted a professional football career, but was one of the last players cut. He joined the Celtics and had a successful 16-year career in the NBA, all with Boston. With the Celtics, 'Hondo' continued the success of the sixth man role. A sixth man is a non-starter who comes off the bench and gives his team a lift. Most sixth men can easily start, but are best coming off the bench.

The 6 ft 5 in forward/guard was named to the All-NBA First Team four times and to the All-NBA Defensive First Team five times. He contributed greatly to eight of the Celtics' NBA Championships. He is in the top five of almost every statistical category: fifth on the career scoring list with 26,395 points; third on most games played with 1270; fourth on minutes played with 46,471; fourth in field goals made with 10,513; and third in field goals attempted with 23,900.

As captain of the Celtics for most of his career, he was a great clutch player. Whenever the team needed a basket, a steal, or a rebound, 'Hondo' was always there to give his team the extra spark they needed. This Hall of Famer was named to the NBA 35th Anniversary All-Time Team.

Elvin Hayes

Opposite: *A quick first step let John Havlicek simply blow by his man. Superb on offense and defense, 'Hondo' ranks fifth in career points. Havlicek rarely rested and had a reputation for being able to run all night.*

Above and right: *Elvin Hayes was a prolific scorer and rebounder. As an NBA rookie, Hayes led the league with 28.4 points a game. He retired 15 years later, third in career points.*

Elvin Hayes was a hard-working player with all the right tools – he could shoot, rebound, and play defense. While at the University of Houston, the three-time All-American averaged 31 points per game. The Cougars made 1967 and 1968 Final Four appearances, and the 1968 College Player-of-the-Year averaged 36.8 points per game during his senior year.

He was the number one pick in the 1968 NBA draft by the San Diego Rockets. In 16 NBA seasons (1969-84), Hayes was named to the 1969 All-NBA Rookie Team, named to the All-NBA First Team three times, named to the All-NBA Second Team three times, and made the All-NBA Defensive Second Team twice. As a rookie, he led the league in scoring with an average of

28.4 points per game. He led the NBA in rebounding in 1970 and 1974 and played in 12 NBA All-Star games.

The 6ft 9in center is in the top five on many NBA lists: second on most games played with 1303; second on most minutes played with 50,000; fourth on most rebounds with 16,279; fifth on most blocked shots with 1771; third on most field goals made with 10,976; second on most field goals attempted with 24,272; and tied for second in most seasons played with 16. 'The Big E' had a career average of 21 points per game and scored 27,313 points, which places him third on the all-time points scored list. With the Washington Bullets, Hayes played in two NBA World Championships, winning the 1978 title.

Tom Heinsohn

At Holy Cross (1953-56), Tom Heinsohn was All-New England each of his three varsity seasons. The two-time All-American and Academic All-American led Coach 'Buster' Sheary's Crusaders to the 1954 National Invitational Tournament (NIT) Championship and was named to the All-NIT team. The team captain had a career average of 22.1 points per game. As a first round draft choice of the Boston Celtics, the 6 ft 7 in forward was the 1957 NBA Rookie-of-the-Year, a starter on eight NBA Championship teams from 1957 to 1965, and appeared in six NBA All-Star games. In 654 regular-season games, he averaged 18.6 points and had 5749 rebounds.

The Hall of Famer went on to become the Celtics' coach in 1970 and compiled a record of 427 and 263 in regular-season play, and 47 and 33 in the playoffs. He coached the Celtics to two NBA crowns, in 1974 and 1976.

Nat Holman

Nat Holman was graduated from Commerce High School in New York City in 1916, having played four sports. He attended the Savage School of Physical Education and New York University. In 1916 he was picked to play for Hoboken, New Jersey, and in one game scored 23 points in a 28-25 win. Until 1920 he starred for the professional teams in Bridgeport, Scranton, and Germantown and for the New York Whirlwinds. From 1920 through 1928, Holman led the Original Celtics as a great shooter, fine team player, and exceptional ball-handler and passer. He later starred for Syracuse and Chicago.

This 5 ft 11 in Hall of Famer retired from playing in 1933 to concentrate on his coaching career at the City College of New York. He had begun coaching CCNY while still a student in 1919, and continued for 41 years until his retirement in 1960. In 1950 his 'Cinderella' CCNY Beavers won both the NIT and NCAA titles, a feat never before accomplished.

Right: *Nat Holman sparked the Original Celtics in the 1920s with his shooting and passing.*

Opposite: *Rugged forward Tom Heinsohn scores inside on the Royals. He was a steady performer on eight championship Boston teams.*

Lou Hudson

At the University of Minnesota, Lou Hudson averaged 20.4 points per game and was a 1965 All-American. The St. Louis Hawks drafted him on the fourth pick of the 1966 NBA draft. In 13 seasons, he played for the St. Louis/Atlanta Hawks and the Los Angeles Lakers. Hudson was named to the 1967 All-NBA Rookie Team and to the 1970 All-NBA Second Team. He played in six NBA All-Star games.

The 6ft 5in forward was known as a great scorer and averaged 20.2 points per game with 17,940 career points, which places him 25th on the all-time list. He had his best year in 1973, when he averaged 27.1 points per game. Hudson played his career in obscurity. His teams never made a serious run for the NBA World Championship.

Opposite: *A mobile forward with smooth moves, Lou Hudson was selected for six NBA All-Star games.*

Right: *'Sweet Lou' looks for an opening.*

Dan Issel

Dan Issel, a two-time All-American, averaged 25.8 points per game at the University of Kentucky. The Kentucky Colonels of the American Basketball Association selected him in the first round of the 1970 ABA draft. In six ABA seasons (1971-76), five with Kentucky and one with Denver, he was named the 1971 ABA Rookie-of-the-Year, named to the 1972 All-ABA First Team, and named to the All-ABA Second Team four times. Issel had an average of 25.6 points per game and led the league in scoring in 1971. He set an ABA record for most points in a season with 2538 in 1972. The 6ft 9in center played in six ABA All-Star games and was named the 1972 game MVP. Issel led the Colonels to the 1975 ABA Championship.

In 1976 the ABA merged with the NBA and Issel played nine NBA seasons (1977-85), all with the Denver Nuggets. He averaged 20.4 points per game and played in one NBA All-Star game. His combined ABA/NBA statistics would place him fourth in career points scored with 27,482 (however, the NBA recognizes only NBA statistics). Issel remains one of the most consistent scorers in the history of basketball.

Right: *Dan Issel could shoot from inside and afar. In the NBA he averaged 20.4 points per game.*

Dennis Johnson

Dennis Johnson attended Los Angeles Harbor Junior College (1974-75) and Pepperdine University (1976). At Pepperdine, he played one year and averaged 15.7 points per game. The Seattle Supersonics drafted him as a hardship case in the second round of the 1976 draft.

A defensive specialist, 'DJ' has a knack for playing in the NBA Championship series. Since 1977, he has played on three teams and in six NBA Finals. Johnson was a member of the 1979 Seattle World Championship team and the 1984 and 1986 Boston World Championship teams. In 1979 he was named the NBA Playoff MVP. The 6 ft 4 in guard was named to the 1981 All-NBA First Team, named to the 1980 All-NBA Second Team, named to the All-NBA Defensive First Team six times, and named to the All-NBA Defensive Second Team three times. Johnson has played in five NBA All-Star games.

Earvin Johnson, Jr

Left and below: *Magic Johnson has a step on his man and that's all he needs. Magic's brilliant passing – he has 1800 playoff assists – triggers the Lakers' potent offense.*

During the 1980 Championship series Kareem Abdul-Jabbar got hurt as the Philadelphia 76ers were playing the Los Angeles Lakers. The Lakers did not have a backup center. Coach Pat Riley moved his 6ft 9in rookie Earvin Johnson from his familiar point guard position to center. He then scored 42 points as the Lakers wrapped up the title.

In two seasons at Michigan State University, the 1979 All-American averaged 17.1 points per game. The Spartans won the 1979 NCAA Championship and Johnson was named the Tournament's Most Outstanding Player. He was drafted as the first pick by the Los Angeles Lakers in the 1979 draft as an undergraduate.

In nine years of 'Magic' Johnson, the Lakers have become the dominant team of the 1980s. Since 1980 they have won five NBA Championships (1980, 1982, 1985, 1987, and 1988) and were runner-up in 1984. As a rookie he won an NBA title, making him one of a handful of players to win an NCAA and NBA title in back-to-back seasons.

In nine seasons Johnson has been named to the 1980 All-NBA Rookie Team, named to the All-NBA First Team six times, and the 1982 All-NBA Second Team. He was named the Playoff MVP three times, the 1987 NBA MVP, and recipient of the 1984 Schick Pivotal Player Award. 'Magic' holds the all-time NBA playoff record for most assists with 1800 and the Championship series record for most assists in a game with 24. He led the league in steals twice and in assists four times. Johnson has a career average of 19.1 points per game and a playoff average of 19.0. In eight NBA All-Star games, he holds the record for most assists in one game with 22 and the record for most assists with 111. Johnson is truly a franchise player who has brought a new look to NBA backcourt play.

Neil Johnston

Neil Johnston played two years at Ohio State University (1947-48) but signed a professional baseball contract in 1948 which made him ineligible for his final two years of college basketball.

The Philadelphia Warriors signed him as a free agent in 1951. Although Johnston only played eight NBA seasons (1952-59), all with Philadelphia, he was one of the most feared scorers of his era. He was named to the All-NBA First Team four times and the 1957 All-NBA Second Team. At 6ft 8in, he led the league in scoring for three consecutive years and led the NBA in field goal percentage three times. Wilt Chamberlain and Johnston are the only two players to lead the league in both scoring and rebounding in a single season. Johnston accomplished this in 1955. The Warriors won the NBA Championship in 1956 as Neil averaged 20.3 points per game during the playoffs. He played in six NBA All-Star games. Johnston finished his basketball career with an average of 19.4 points per game.

K.C. Jones

K.C. Jones was a role player who, wherever he played, a championship followed. He and Bill Russell created the University of San Francisco and the Boston Celtics Championship dynasties. At San Francisco (1952-56), he averaged 8.8 points per game and, along with Russell, led the Dons to the 1955 and 1956 NCAA Championships. He was a member of the 1956 gold medal U.S. Olympic team.

The Boston Celtics picked him in the second round of the 1956 draft. His professional career was interrupted by military service for two seasons. Upon returning to Boston for the 1959 season, he played nine seasons with the Celtics (1959-67). An important factor in eight consecutive NBA Championships (1959-66), the 6ft 1in guard averaged 7.4 points per game during his career. This Hall of Famer also coached the Celtics to the 1984 and 1986 NBA titles.

Opposite: *At 6ft 9in, Johnson is tough to stop near the basket or when he flicks a pass. Magic has guided Los Angeles to five NBA titles in the 1980s.*

Top: *Neil Johnston takes a hook shot in 1957.*

Right: *A solid defender, K.C. Jones often drew the opponent's star guard.*

Sam Jones

At North Carolina Central College (NAIA), Sam Jones averaged 17.7 points per game. He took two years off from college for military service. He was a collegiate unknown but was the number one draft choice of the Boston Celtics in 1957. He played 12 NBA seasons (1958-69) and turned out to be one of the greatest Celtics of all time.

Jones averaged 17.7 points per game during his professional career. The 6 ft 4 in guard was selected to three All-NBA Second Teams and played in five NBA All-Star games. This Hall of Famer played on ten World Championship teams with the Celtics. In 154 playoff games, he averaged 18.9 points per game. Jones was named to the National Association of Intercollegiate Athletics (NAIA) Basketball Hall of Fame in 1962, named to the NBA 25th Anniversary All-Time Team in 1970, and elected in 1983 to the Naismith Memorial Basketball Hall of Fame.

Michael Jordan

One of the most dynamic players of the 1980s, Michael Jordan was drafted by the Chicago Bulls in the first round of the 1984 draft as an undergraduate. At the University of North Carolina (1982-84), the two-time College Player-of-the-Year averaged 17.7 points per game. In 1982, Jordan helped the Tarheels to an NCAA Division I Championship. The two-time All-American led the U.S. Olympic team to the 1984 gold medal.

In four NBA seasons, Jordan has become the most exciting, popular player in the game. He was named

Left: *Michael Jordan contests a shot by Bernard King. The complete player, Jordan led the NBA in scoring in 1988 and was Defensive Player-of-the-Year.*

Opposite: *Sam Jones on the move and driving off a Bill Russell pick in 1965. Jones's shooting helped the Celtics win 10 NBA crowns.*

Page 62: *In the 1982 NCAA Championship game, Jordan hit the shot that won it for North Carolina. He has been on the rise ever since.*

the 1985 NBA Rookie-of-the-Year, made the 1985 All-NBA Second Team, made the All-NBA First Team twice, and was the recipient of the 1985 Schick Pivotal Player Award. The 6 ft 6 in guard has led the league in scoring for two consecutive years (1987 and 1988) and in steals once (1988). In 1988, Jordan took home a majority of the awards: NBA MVP, NBA Defensive Player-of-the-Year, and NBA All-Star game MVP. Due to injury he only played in 18 games during the 1986 season, but he still set the NBA playoff game record for most points with 63. Since 1985, he has averaged 32.7 points per game, and in 20 playoff games has averaged 35.9. He has played in three All-Star games. He is known for his acrobatic style.

Bob Kurland

Bob Kurland was graduated from Jennings High School in St. Louis, Missouri in 1942 and Oklahoma State University in 1946. The first of the truly great seven-footers, Kurland wrote basketball history in leading his Oklahoma State teams to successive NCAA titles in 1945 and 1946. He was the national scoring leader in 1946 and MVP of the 1945 and 1946 NCAA Tournament. Elected to every All-America team in 1946, Kurland joined the Amateur Athletic Union (AAU) Phillips Oilers in 1946 and was selected All-League and All-AAU for each of the six years he played. A member of the 1948 and 1952 gold medal U.S. Olympic teams, the Hall of Famer was selected by Grantland Rice to the All-Time All-American Team.

Below and below right: *Bob Lanier was a space-eater who scored 20 points a game.*

Right: *Bob Kurland, shooting for the Oilers, starred in the AAU for six seasons.*

Bob Lanier

At St. Bonaventure University (1968-70), Bob Lanier averaged 27.6 points per game during his college career. The two-time collegiate All-American was drafted by the Detroit Pistons as the number one pick of the 1970 draft. In 14 NBA seasons (1971-84), he played nine-and-a-half years with Detroit and four-and-a-half with Milwaukee. During his professional career, Lanier averaged 20.0 points per game and scored 19,248 points, which places him 16th on the all-time list. He is the number one left-handed scorer in NBA history. He was named to the 1971 All-NBA Rookie Team, played in eight NBA All-Star games and was named the 1974 game MVP. Throughout his 14-year career he never played on a championship team. The 6ft 11in center was a great scorer and rebounder. Lanier was also known for his size 22 sneakers, the largest in basketball.

Joe Lapchick

Joe Lapchick began playing professional basketball at the age of 17 without a high school education, as his immigrant parents needed his support. Attracted by his agility and 6ft 5in frame, great teams sought him and for 19 years, from 1917 to 1936, this Hall of Famer was the best center of his time. Among the teams he played for were Holyoke in the Western Massachusetts League, the Brooklyn Visitations in the Metropolitan League, and Troy of the New York State League. He was the center of the immortal Original Celtics from 1923 to 1927, when they never lost a series.

When the American Basketball League disbanded the Celtics, Lapchick played for an extended tour, from 1930 to 1936, before becoming one of America's foremost coaches at St. John's University and then for the New York Knickerbockers in the NBA.

Opposite: *Nancy Lieberman brings the ball up court.*

Right: *Joe Lapchick, a pro at the age of 17, became the best center of his era.*

Nancy Lieberman

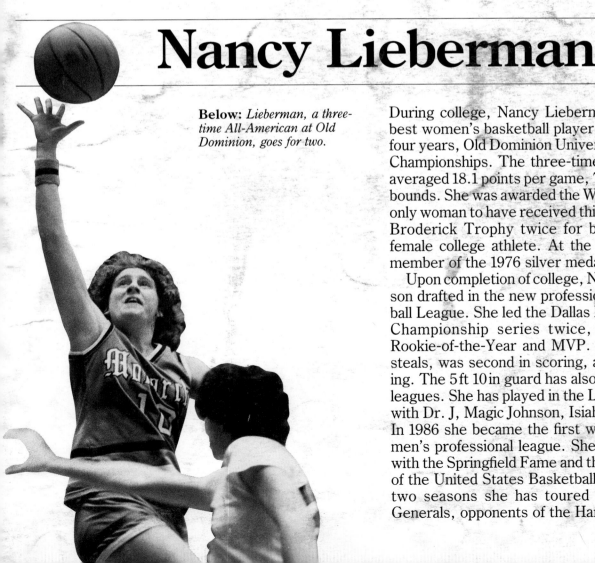

Below: *Lieberman, a three-time All-American at Old Dominion, goes for two.*

During college, Nancy Lieberman was hailed as the best women's basketball player in the country. In her four years, Old Dominion University won two National Championships. The three-time Kodak All-American averaged 18.1 points per game, 7.2 assists, and 8.7 rebounds. She was awarded the Wade Trophy twice (the only woman to have received this award twice) and the Broderick Trophy twice for being the outstanding female college athlete. At the age of 16, she was a member of the 1976 silver medal U.S. Olympic team.

Upon completion of college, Nancy was the first person drafted in the new professional Women's Basketball League. She led the Dallas Diamonds to the WBL Championship series twice, was named All-Pro Rookie-of-the-Year and MVP. She led the league in steals, was second in scoring, and fourth in rebounding. The 5ft 10in guard has also played in many men's leagues. She has played in the Lakers' summer league with Dr. J, Magic Johnson, Isiah Thomas, and others. In 1986 she became the first woman to compete in a men's professional league. She played a season each with the Springfield Fame and the Long Island Knights of the United States Basketball League. For the past two seasons she has toured with the Washington Generals, opponents of the Harlem Globetrotters.

Clyde Lovellette

At the University of Kansas, where he played three years for Hall of Fame Coach 'Phog' Allen, Clyde Lovellette was a three-time All-American (1950-52), was Big Seven scoring champion each season, and led the nation in scoring with a 28.4 average. In his senior year, as captain, the 6 ft 9 in center led the Jayhawks to the NCAA title and was named Tournament MVP. The College Player-of-the-Year was a member of the 1952 gold medal U.S. Olympic team in Helsinki. In 1952-53, he played with the Phillips Oilers, champions of the National Industrial Basketball League (NIBL) with a 50-5 record. He scored 944 points, and was named to the NIBL All-Star Team.

During his 11 seasons in the NBA (1954-66), the Hall of Famer played with the 1954 champion Minneapolis Lakers and the 1963 and 1964 champion Boston Celtics. He played four years with the Lakers, one with Cincinnati, four with St. Louis, and wound up his career in 1964 after two seasons with the Celtics. Lovellette averaged 17 points per game in 704 NBA games.

Right: *Clyde Lovellette won College Player-of-the-Year honors at Kansas in 1952 and went on to play 11 seasons in the NBA.*

Jerry Lucas

Jerry Lucas was considered one of the greatest college players of all time. During his college career, he was one of only seven players to average over 20 points and 20 rebounds per game in the NCAA. In three years at Ohio State, Lucas was a complete player. He led the NCAA in field goal percentage for three years and in rebounds for his last two years. With Lucas, the Buckeyes reached the NCAA Division I Finals in each of his three years, winning the title in 1960. He was named College Player-of-the-Year in 1960 and 1961. He was also honored as the NCAA Tournament Most Outstanding Player in 1960 and 1961. Lucas was named All-American for three years at Ohio State. Lucas averaged 17 points per game as a member of the 1960 gold medal U.S. Olympic team during his sophomore year.

The 6 ft 8 in forward was drafted by the Cincinnati Royals in the first round, but decided to sign with Cleveland of the American Basketball League (ABL). Before Lucas even played a game, Cleveland folded, so he did not play pro ball in that first year. In 1963, he signed with the Royals. During his 11-year NBA career, with three teams, he won one NBA Championship as a member of the New York Knicks in 1973. He was honored as the NBA Rookie-of-the-Year with Cincinnati in 1964 and made the All-NBA First Team three times. Lucas played in seven NBA All-Star games and was named game MVP in 1965 as he scored 25 points. As a rookie, he led the NBA in field goal percentage. For his professional career, the Hall of Famer had an average of 17.0 points and 15.6 rebounds per game.

Above: *An All-American at Ohio State, Lucas averaged over 20 points and 20 rebounds a game for his college career – only six others have achieved this mark.*

Left: *Jerry Lucas turns the corner on Tom Heinsohn in 1965. Luke's steady play put him on the All-NBA First Team three times.*

Hank Luisetti

Hank Luisetti never played in a college tournament or played professional basketball, but he will go down in history as the player that revolutionized basketball. Hank invented a new form of putting the ball in the basket – the one-handed shot.

At Stanford University (1935-38), he averaged 16.8 points per game and scored 1596 career points in 95 games. The two-time All-American became the very first college player to score 50 points in a game. The 6 ft 2 in guard led the Cardinals to three straight Pacific Coast Conference titles and was voted second behind George Mikan as the 'greatest player in the first half-century' by AP. Following college, he began playing Amateur Athletic Union (AAU) ball. He was AAU First Team All-America twice and finished with a career total of 2997 points.

Ed Macauley

Ed Macauley began his basketball career at St. Louis University, graduating in 1945. At St. Louis, he became one of the Billikens' great players, and was named All-American. He was named the Associated Press Player-of-the-Year his senior year. At the 1948 National Invitational Tournament, this Hall of Famer was named MVP as the Billikens won the Championship. He averaged 13.6 points per game as a collegiate player, an impressive figure for those years.

The 6 ft 8 in forward/center was drafted by the St. Louis Bombers in the first round of the Basketball Association of America (BAA) draft. In August of 1949, the BAA merged with the NBL to form the NBA. In a

total of ten NBA seasons, one with the St. Louis Bombers, six with the Boston Celtics, and three with the St. Louis Hawks, he averaged 17.5 points per game as a professional. Macauley played in the first seven NBA All-Star games and holds the honor of being named the first game MVP in 1951. He was named to the All-NBA First Team three times. In 1954, he led the NBA in field goal percentage. He won one NBA Championship, in 1958 with the Hawks.

Known for his soft shooting touch, 'Easy Ed' Macauley will always be remembered as one of the players traded to the Hawks, thus bringing Bill Russell to Boston to help build the Celtics dynasty.

Moses Malone

Moses Malone did not attend college and came right out of Petersburgh High School in Virginia into professional basketball. The Utah Stars signed him as an undergraduate in the third round of the 1974 American Basketball Association (ABA) draft. In two seasons of ABA basketball, one with Utah and one with St. Louis, Malone was named to the 1975 All-ABA Rookie Team and played in the 1975 ABA All-Star game.

During the ABA/NBA merger, he was drafted by Portland, traded to Buffalo and then traded to Houston in 1976. In 12 NBA seasons (six with Houston, four with Philadelphia, and two with Washington), Malone was named to the All-NBA First Team four times, the All-NBA Second Team four times, and the 1979 All-NBA Defensive Second Team. He has led the league in rebounding six times and was the NBA's MVP three times. He was selected to play in 11 NBA All-Star games. In 1981 he led the Rockets all the way to the NBA Finals before losing to the Celtics in six games. With the 76ers he finally won a Championship in 1983 and was named the Playoff MVP.

The 6ft 10in center averaged 23.6 points per game and has scored 21,703 career points which places him eighth on the all-time list. He has averaged 23.2 points per game in 84 NBA playoff games. He is tenth on the all-time rebound list with 12,715, fourth in free throws made with 6636, and fifth in free throws attempted with 8692.

Danny Manning

Based on his college performance alone we have to include Danny Manning on our list of 100 greatest players. At the University of Kansas the 1987 and 1988 First Team All-American and 1986 Second Team All-American scored 2951 career points for an average of 20.1 points per game. During his senior year he averaged 24.8 points per game in leading the Jayhawks to a 'Cinderella' season and to the NCAA Championship. Manning was named the Most Outstanding Player in the NCAA Division I Tournament. The 6ft 10in center was drafted number one by the Los Angeles Clippers in the 1988 draft. His pro potential is unlimited. He is the son of Ed Manning, a professional player from 1968 to 1976.

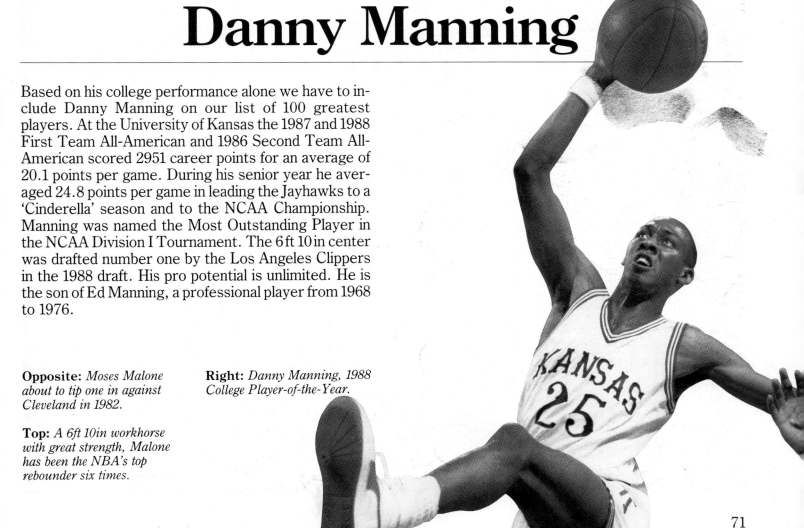

Opposite: *Moses Malone about to tip one in against Cleveland in 1982.*

Top: *A 6ft 10in workhorse with great strength, Malone has been the NBA's top rebounder six times.*

Right: *Danny Manning, 1988 College Player-of-the-Year.*

Pete Maravich

Pete Maravich was the greatest scorer in the history of college basketball. While at Louisiana State University, he played for his father, Press, and turned the school into a national powerhouse. In three years of varsity play, 'Pistol' in his famous floppy socks set many scoring records including his total of 3667 points. He averaged 44.2 points per game during his college career. He is the only player in history to average over 40 points per game. To appreciate what an incredible feat this was, consider that the second-place player averaged 34.6 points per game.

A three-time First Team All-America selection and College Player-of-the-Year in 1970, Maravich led the nation in scoring in his three years. 'Pistol Pete' rewrote the NCAA career and season record books. He scored at least 50 points a game 28 times, had most field goals made with 1387, and most field goals attempted with 3166. Maravich set season records for most points (1381), highest scoring average (44.5), most field goals made (522), and most field goals attempted (1168).

The Atlanta Hawks drafted Maravich on the third pick of the first round in 1970. He played ten NBA seasons with four teams. In 1977, he led the NBA in scoring with 2273 points and had a career average of 24.2 points per game. He played in four NBA All-Star games.

The 6 ft 5 in Hall of Fame guard will always be remembered as one of those great players who never won a championship. His playing style of dazzling passes and shots that defied gravity will be matched by no one. He will go down in history as one of the flashiest players ever to play the game of basketball.

Slater Martin

The smallest super-player in NBA history, Slater Martin excelled in professional basketball because of his talent and desire. He could shoot and pass, but his fame was as a defensive genius and team leader. The 5 ft 10 in guard was drafted by the Minneapolis Lakers in 1949 out of the University of Texas where he once scored 49 points in one game, a record for the Southwest Conference that still stands today. In his 11 NBA seasons (seven with Minneapolis and four with St. Louis), 'Dugie' played in seven consecutive NBA All-Star games and was a member of five championship teams – four with the Lakers and one with the Hawks. He was named to the All-NBA Second Team five times.

Opposite: *Pete Maravich lit up arenas with his shooting and passing.*

Top: *'The Pistol' in the open court was hard to defend.*

Right: *A 5ft 10in floor general and skilled defender, Slater Martin played on five NBA Championship teams.*

Bob McAdoo

Bob McAdoo attended Vincennes University and the University of North Carolina. In one year at North Carolina, the 1972 All-American averaged 19.5 points per game. The Buffalo Braves drafted him second in the 1972 draft as a hardship case. McAdoo was a fantastic scorer, but was an NBA journeyman. He played for seven NBA teams in 14 seasons (1973-86). His credentials are impressive: 1973 NBA Rookie-of-the-Year, 1975 NBA MVP, 1975 All-NBA First Team,

1974 All-NBA Second Team, led the league in scoring for three consecutive years, and led in field goal percentage in 1974. He played in five NBA All-Star games.

The 6 ft 9 in forward averaged 22.1 points per game and scored 18,787 points during his career, which places him 19th on the all-time scoring list. As a sixth man, he helped the Los Angeles Lakers to four straight NBA Finals and contributed to the 1982 and 1985 titles.

Bobby McDermott

Known as 'The Little Man,' the 5 ft 11 in set-shot expert turned professional after his first year at Flushing (New York) High School. During an illustrious 17-year professional career, Bobby McDermott was voted 'the greatest professional basketball player of all time' by coaches and managers in the National Basketball League (1945). He was selected as an NBL All-Star for seven straight years (1942-48); was MVP for five consecutive years (1942-46); and led the league in scoring twice (1943 and 1944). McDermott led the Brooklyn Visitations to the ABL title in 1935. From 1936 to 1939 he played for the Original Celtics. He led the Fort Wayne Zollner Pistons to three straight NBL titles from 1944 to 1946 during his five years with Fort Wayne. In 1947 he led the Chicago Gears to the NBL Championship as a player-coach. He wound up his career in 1950 and was named to the All-World Team by *Collier's Magazine*. In 1954 this Hall of Famer was voted the 'greatest Fort Wayne Zollner player of all time.' McDermott was considered the dominant player in professional basketball from the mid-1930s through the late 1940s. He died in an automobile accident in 1963.

Opposite: *Even with a hand in his face, Bob McAdoo could get off his shot. His offensive prowess led to three NBA scoring titles.*

Right: *Bobby McDermott at 5ft 11in was a force in the pro game from 1935 to 1948, earning five MVP awards.*

Above: *McAdoo drives the baseline.*

George McGinnis

In his one year of college basketball at Indiana University, George McGinnis averaged 30 points per game and was an All-American. The Indiana Pacers of the American Basketball Association (ABA) signed him as an undergraduate free agent in 1971. With the Pacers, McGinnis was named to the 1972 All-ABA Rookie Team, named to the 1973 All-ABA Second Team, named to the 1974 and 1975 All-ABA First Team, was named the 1975 ABA co-MVP, and led the league in scoring once. He averaged 24.8 points per game in four seasons (1972-75). The Pacers won the 1972 and 1973 ABA Championships, and McGinnis was named the Playoff MVP in 1973. He played in three ABA All-Star games.

The 6ft 8in forward signed with the Philadelphia 76ers of the NBA in 1975. In seven NBA seasons (1976-82), with three different teams, he averaged 17.2 points per game. McGinnis was named to the 1976 All-NBA First Team and the 1977 All-NBA Second Team. He helped lead the 76ers to the 1977 NBA Final but lost to Portland. He also performed in three NBA All-Star games. McGinnis will be remembered best for his unique one-handed jump shot, which was extremely accurate.

Kevin McHale

At the University of Minnesota (1977-80), Kevin McHale averaged 15.2 points per game. The Boston Celtics surprised everybody by drafting him third in the 1980 draft. McHale has turned out to be an outstanding pro player. In eight professional seasons, all with the Celtics, he has been named to the 1981 All-NBA Rookie Team, named to the All-NBA Defensive First Team three times, named to the 1983 All-NBA Defensive Second Team, named to the 1987 All-NBA First Team, led the league in field goal percentage twice, and was the recipient of the NBA Sixth Man Award which goes to the best non-starter for two consecutive years. He has played in four NBA All-Star games.

The lanky 6 ft 10 in forward has averaged 18 points per game and in 1987 alone averaged 26.1 points per game. The Celtics have reached the NBA Finals five times during his career, winning the title in 1981, 1984, and 1986. In 136 NBA playoff games, he has averaged 18.7 points per game.

McHale is known as a good shooter, and his trademark is his soft touch. He is also known as an extremely effective defensive player, where his unusually long arm span comes in handy.

Opposite left: *George McGinnis goes full throttle to the basket.*

Opposite right: *McGinnis powers through the defense. He averaged 24.8 points a game in four years with the Pacers.*

Right: *Good defense and an 18-points-per-game average make Kevin McHale a major contributor to the Celtics' success in the 1980s.*

Ann Meyers

Ann Meyers began her athletic career playing boys' basketball in elementary school. In junior high school she played five sports – basketball, volleyball, track and field, soccer, and softball. In 1970 she was named Female Athlete-of-the-Year. During her high school career she played seven sports and was named MVP for four years in basketball.

The four-time All-American at UCLA also lettered in track and field and volleyball. She led the Bruins to the AIAW National Championship in basketball. She was named the recipient of the Broderick Cup as the nation's Most Outstanding Collegiate Female Athlete.

Meyers was a member of numerous U.S. National Women's Basketball teams that have competed throughout the world. She was a member of the 1975 gold medal Pan American team, a star on the 1976 silver medal U.S. Olympic team, captain of the 1979 silver medal Pan American team, and captain of the 1979 gold medal teams at the World Championship Games and the Jones Cup Tournament.

As a member of the Women's Basketball League's New Jersey Gems, she received the 1978-79 co-Most Valuable Player Award. In 1979, the 5 ft 9 in guard became the first and only woman to sign a contract to try out with an NBA team – the Indiana Pacers. A superb athlete, Ann Meyers has revolutionized the game of women's basketball.

Right: *Ann Meyers, a four-time All-American at UCLA, played tough defense.*

Opposite: *With his hook shot and rebounding, George Mikan was the first big man to dominate in the pros. Over nine seasons, the 6 ft 10 in center averaged 22.6 points a game.*

George Mikan

The greatest player of the 1940s and 1950s, George Mikan was the first-ever dominant big man in the pro ranks. He was also a complete all-around player as he could both shoot and play defense. He began his professional career with the Chicago Gears of the National Basketball League in 1946 and helped them win the Championship. A year later, Mikan signed with the Minneapolis Lakers of the NBL which merged with the BAA, a forerunner of the NBA. With the Lakers, he won one NBL Championship and five NBA World Championships. He played in the first four NBA All-Star games and was named game MVP in 1953. During his nine-year career, he averaged 22.6 points per game, was named to the All-NBA First Team six times, led the league in scoring for three years, and led in rebounding once.

The 6 ft 10 in center began his career at DePaul University where he averaged 19.1 points per game. Mikan helped the Blue Demons to the 1945 National Invitational Tournament Championship and took home the MVP award. The three-time All-American and two-time College Player-of-the-Year led the nation in scoring in 1945 and 1946.

Voted the 'greatest player in the first half-century' by AP, the Hall of Famer was named to the NBA 25th and 35th Anniversary All-Time Teams.

Earl Monroe

Earl Monroe averaged 26.7 points per game during his college career at Winston-Salem State University. The two-time All-American led the 1967 NCAA Division II in scoring where he averaged an incredible 41.5 points per game. He holds the Division II record for most points scored in a season with 1329. Monroe was a member of the 1967 Division II Championship team and was honored as the Most Outstanding Player of the tournament.

The Baltimore Bullets drafted him as the number two pick of the 1967 draft. In 13 NBA seasons (1968-

80), he played with Baltimore and New York. He was named the 1968 NBA Rookie-of-the-Year and was also named to the 1969 All-NBA First Team. He played in four NBA All-Star games. Monroe led the Bullets to the 1971 NBA Finals but the team eventually lost to Milwaukee. With the Knicks, he was a member of the 1973 NBA Championship team. 'The Pearl' averaged 18.8 points per game and scored 17,454 career points, which places him 29th on the all-time points scored list. The 6ft 3in guard was a complete player and was a master of the one-on-one.

Calvin Murphy

Calvin Murphy was an over-achiever. Throughout his career he was said to be too small to survive in the NBA. He survived for 13 seasons. The San Diego Rockets drafted him on the second round of the 1970 draft out of Niagara University. The two-time All-American averaged 33.1 points per game (fourth on the all-time NCAA Division I scoring average list) and 2548 points.

In 13 NBA seasons, all with the Rockets franchise (one with San Diego, 12 with Houston), Murphy was named to the 1971 All-NBA Rookie Team and played in the 1979 NBA All-Star game. As one of the smallest guards in modern NBA history at 5ft 9in, he averaged 17.9 points per game and 17,949 career points. He was one of the greatest free throw shooters ever to play the game, with a career average of .892 (the second highest in NBA history). He led the league in free throw percentage in 1981 and 1983. With a percentage of .958, he holds the NBA record for the highest free throw percentage in one season. Murphy holds the NBA record for most consecutive free throws made with 78.

Opposite: *Earl Monroe shown in a favorite spot on the floor. He would turn his back to the basket, work in a little closer, then whirl and fire off a jumper without seeming to look at the hoop. The shot was usually good. 'The Pearl' had 17,454 career points.*

Left: *Calvin Murphy needed only the slightest opening to penetrate a defense.*

Above: *A 5ft 9in guard, Murphy averaged 17.9 points a game and, for his career, shot 89 percent from the foul line.*

Akeem Olajuwon

A native of Lagos, Nigeria, Akeem Olajuwon attended the University of Houston (1982-84). In his three years of varsity, he led Houston to the NCAA Division I Final Four but could never come away with the Championship. The 1984 All-American averaged 13.3 points per game and 10.7 rebounds per game. Akeem was named the 1983 NCAA Division I Tournament Most Outstanding Player and led the division in field goal percentage, rebounding, and blocked shots in 1984.

The Houston Rockets drafted him number one in 1984 as an undergraduate. He was named to the 1985 All-NBA Rookie Team, to the All-NBA First Team twice, to the 1986 All-NBA Second Team, to the All-NBA Defensive First Team twice, and the 1985 All-NBA Defensive Second Team. He has played in four All-Star games. With the Rockets, the 7ft 0in center has averaged 22.5 points and 11.7 rebounds per game. He led Houston to the 1986 NBA Finals but they eventually lost to Boston in six games. 'Akeem the Dream' is a consistent scorer and rebounder.

Bob Pettit

As the pride of St. Louis, Bob Pettit was a great scorer and great rebounder. He was one of three players to lead the league in rebounding and scoring in the same year. The three-time All-American was drafted on the first round in 1954 by the Milwaukee Hawks out of Louisiana State University, where he averaged 27.4 points per game. In 11 NBA seasons (one with Milwaukee, ten with St. Louis), he was named NBA Rookie-of-the-Year, named to the All-NBA First Team ten times, and named to the All-NBA Second Team once. He played in 11 NBA All-Star games and was named game MVP in 1956, 1958, and 1962, and co-MVP in 1959. Pettit holds the All-Star game record for most rebounds in one game with 27 and is third on the all-time All-Star game scoring list with 224 points.

The 6ft 9in forward led the NBA in scoring in 1956 and 1959 and rebounding in 1956. His career average of 26.4 points is the fourth best in the NBA. He led the St. Louis Hawks to an NBA Championship title in 1958 and as runners-up in 1957, 1959, 1960, and 1961. The Hall of Famer retired in 1965 as the then-highest scorer in NBA history with 20,880 points. He ended his brilliant career by being named to the NBA 25th and 35th Anniversary All-Time Teams.

Opposite: *Akeem Olajuwon follows through on a shot against Louisville in the 1983 NCAA tourney. Strength and agility mark 'The Dream's' game.*

Right: *Bob Pettit was a First Team All-NBA pick ten times. In 1956 he led the league in scoring and rebounding.*

Andy Phillip

At the University of Illinois, Andy Phillip was a member of the fabulous Illinois 'Whiz Kids.' The two-time All-American averaged 12 points per game during his college career. The 1943 College Player-of-the-Year set Big Ten scoring records in 1942 and 1943 as his team won consecutive conference titles. His college career was then interrupted by three years of military service.

The Chicago Stags of the Basketball Association of America (BAA) drafted him in 1947. In 11 seasons in the BAA and NBA (1948-58), he played with four different teams – the Chicago Stags, the Philadelphia Warriors, the Fort Wayne Pistons, and the Boston Celtics. The 6 ft 2 in guard was named to the All-NBA Second Team twice, led the league in assists twice, and played in five NBA All-Star games. The Pistons were runners-up in 1955 and 1956 but Phillip finally won a Championship in 1957 with the Celtics. The Hall of Famer averaged 9.1 points per game during his professional career.

Right: *Andy Phillip twice led the NBA in assists.*

Below: *Jim Pollard went from the AAU to the NBA.*

Opposite: *Kevin Porter takes off down the lane. A superb set-up man, Porter won the NBA assists title four times.*

Jim Pollard

Jim Pollard played one season of basketball at Stanford University. The 1942 All-American averaged 10.5 points per game, and was a member of the 1942 NCAA Division I Championship team. His college career was interrupted by military service from 1943 to 1945.

Upon returning, Pollard played in the Amateur Athletic Union (AAU) for two seasons, where he was the leading scorer both times. Minneapolis of the National Basketball League signed him in 1947 and he led them to the 1948 NBL Championship. When Minneapolis merged into the NBA, he continued to play seven seasons (1949-55), all with the Lakers. With Pollard, Minneapolis won five NBA World Championships. The 6 ft 5 in forward was named to the All-NBA First Team twice, named to the All-NBA Second Team twice, and played in the first four NBA All-Star games. This Hall of Famer averaged 13.1 points during his career and 13.6 points during the playoffs. He was a classic team player and was known for his jump shot. Pollard lived in the shadow of George Mikan, so he did not get the recognition he deserved.

Kevin Porter

As one of the best assist men in the NBA, Kevin Porter led the league in assists four times. He holds the record for most assists in one game with 29, is third on the NBA list for most assists in a season with 1099, and has the third highest average for assists per game during a season with 13.4.

The Baltimore Bullets drafted him in the third round of the 1972 draft out of St. Francis College in Pennsylvania (1969-72). He averaged 23.8 points per game with 1712 career points. In ten NBA seasons, the 6 ft 0 in guard helped the Bullets to the 1975 NBA Finals, where they eventually lost to Golden State. He had a professional career average of 11.6 points and 7.1 assists per game.

Frank Ramsey

At the University of Kentucky (1951-54), Frank Ramsey averaged 14.8 points per game. The two-time All-American was a member of the 1951 NCAA Championship team.

The Boston Celtics picked him in the first round of the 1953 draft. Ramsey spent his entire professional career with Boston (1955, 1957-64). He missed the 1955-56 season while he served in the military. The 6 ft 3 in guard perfected the sixth man role. In nine NBA seasons, he averaged 13.4 points per game and 13.6 points in 98 career playoff games. With the Celtics, he was a member of seven NBA Championship teams. Ramsey could have been a star player for any other team, but he enjoyed his role as a substitute for a successful team. The Hall of Famer was a consummate team player and an integral part of the Celtics dynasty.

Right: *Frank Ramsey had the ability to come off the bench and score right away.*

Opposite top: *Willis Reed drives on Bob Ferry.*

Opposite bottom: *Reed shoots his jumper against the Bucks. The heart of the Knicks, Reed won three MVP awards in 1970.*

Willis Reed

The year was 1970. Willis Reed of the New York Knicks had just been named the NBA Playoff MVP and had guided his team to a World Championship to end a brilliant season. He had begun the year by taking home the NBA All-Star game MVP award as he scored 21 points and grabbed 11 rebounds. As the regular NBA season came to a close, Reed was named to the All-NBA First Team, named to the All-NBA Defensive First Team, and named the NBA's MVP. He is the only player ever to be honored as the NBA MVP, NBA All-Star game MVP, and the NBA Playoff MVP in one season.

The 6 ft 10 in center was drafted by the Knicks on the tenth pick of the second round out of Grambling College, where he averaged 18.7 points per game. He had led Grambling to three NAIA Championship games and helped his team to win one title. At the end of his first year in the pros, he was named NBA Rookie-of-the-Year – the only player to win the award who was not drafted in the first round. In ten seasons, all with the Knicks, Reed played in seven NBA All-Star games and was a member of two championship teams. During his NBA career, the Hall of Famer averaged 18.7 points per game.

Oscar Robertson

Perhaps the greatest guard ever to play the game of basketball, Oscar Robertson was a complete player who did everything flawlessly. He was a natural, the ultimate team leader. Robertson was drafted on the first round by the Cincinnati Royals out of the University of Cincinnati. In 14 seasons, he was named NBA Rookie-of-the-Year, named to the All-NBA First Team nine times, led the NBA in assists six times, led the NBA in free throw percentage twice, and was named the league MVP in 1964. For his professional career, the 'Big O' averaged 25.7 points per game and scored 26,710 points, which places him fourth on the all-time points scored list. Robertson ended his career as the all-time NBA leader in assists with 9887 and in free throws made with 7694. With 12 consecutive NBA All-Star game appearances, he is the second all-time leading scorer in total points (246) and first in career average (20.5) in the All-Star games. He played on one NBA Championship team, with the Milwaukee Bucks.

At the University of Cincinnati, the three-time All-American led the NCAA in scoring for three years and played on two NCAA Tournament third place teams. The 6 ft 5 in guard was named College Player-of-the-Year for three consecutive years. He is fourth on the NCAA all-time career scoring list with 2973 points and third on the all-time career scoring average list with 33.8. This Hall of Famer was the first person to lead the nation in scoring three times in a row and when he finished his college career, he was the all-time leading college scorer. Before he began his NBA career, Robertson co-captained the 1960 U.S. Olympic team to a gold medal. To end a brilliant career, he was named to the NBA 35th Anniversary All-Time Team.

Top: *A three-time All-American at Cincinnati, Oscar Robertson's pro career was equally brilliant.*

Right: *The 'Big O' cuts sharply on Sam Jones. With his great scoring and smooth passing, Oscar could simply control a game.*

Opposite: *Oscar lays one in as the Knicks can only watch. In the NBA he averaged 25.7 points a game and is the all-time assists leader.*

88

John Roosma

John Roosma was graduated in 1921 from Passaic High School in New Jersey and the United States Military Academy in 1926. He was named All-State and was the state tournament high scorer all three years in high school. As a member of the 'Wonder Team' that compiled a record 159 victories, Coach Blood called Roosma Passaic's greatest player. At West Point he led the team to an undefeated season and 33 consecutive victories. This Hall of Famer was the first to score over 1000 career points, with 354 points in one season.

A complete player who did everything well on the court, Roosma was called the backbone of the Army team and the outstanding basketball player of the era by General Douglas MacArthur. At 6ft 1in, he led Army to 70 wins against 3 losses over three years. Roosma won the coveted Army Athletic Sabre as outstanding athlete.

Right: *John Roosma was the first college player to score over 1000 career points.*

Below: *Bill Russell protects the ball from the 'Big O.'*

Opposite: *Russell rebounds.*

Bill Russell

Everything Bill Russell touched turned to gold. During his college career at the University of San Francisco, the two-time All-American was one of only seven players to average over 20 points and 20 rebounds per game as he helped USF win two consecutive NCAA Championships. He was named the 1955 NCAA Tournament Most Outstanding Player. The 1956 College Player-of-the-Year capped the 1955-56 season by leading the U.S. Olympic team to a gold medal.

Russell, a 6ft 10in center, entered the NBA as the highest-paid rookie ever in NBA history. The Boston Celtics traded away two of its best players to St. Louis for the draft rights to Russell, who became an integral part of the best franchise in NBA history. The Celtics drafted him with their third pick in the first round of the 1956 draft. In 13 NBA seasons, the 1970 *Sporting News* Athlete-of-the-Decade helped Boston to 11 World Championships, which included eight straight and two as player-coach.

The 1968 *Sports Illustrated* Sportsman-of-the-Year revolutionized the game with his defensive wizardry and outstanding team play. Russell was a rebounding, defensive specialist, second on the all-time rebounding list with 21,620. He led the league in rebounding for

four years, was named to the All-NBA Defensive First Team in 1969, and was the NBA's all-time playoff leader in rebounding with 4104. This Hall of Famer was awarded the NBA MVP award five times and named to the All-NBA First Team three times. In 12 consecutive NBA All-Star game appearances, he was named the game MVP in 1963. During his professional career, he was selected the 'Greatest Player in the History of the NBA' by the Basketball Writers of America. He averaged 22.3 rebounds and 15.1 points per game and was named to the NBA 25th and 35th Anniversary All-Time Teams.

John Russell

Left: *John Russell, a defensive star.*

John Russell was graduated in 1919 from Alexander Hamilton High School in Brooklyn, New York; Seton Hall University in 1936; and New York University in 1938. While in high school, 'Honey' began a 28-year professional career during which he played in every major pro league, gaining acclaim as the top defensive player of his era. In over 3200 games, this Hall of Famer played some of the sport's great individual scorers. At 6 ft 1 in he led many teams to championships, including five straight titles from 1925 to 1929 with the Cleveland Rosenblums. As player-coach for 20 years, Russell was selected All-League from 1926 to 1929. In 1947 he became the first coach of the NBA's Boston Celtics.

Below: *Dolph Schayes played 15 years in the NBA, scoring 19.2 points a game.*

Opposite: *Schayes led the NBA in free throw percentage for three seasons.*

Dolph Schayes

Dolph Schayes was known as an 'ironman.' He rarely missed a game in 16 professional seasons. During his pro career he played in 1059 regular-season games, and from February 1952 to December 1961 he played in 765 consecutive games.

The All-American at New York University was drafted by Tri-Cities of the National Basketball League (NBL), but his draft rights were then traded to Syracuse of the same league. He played in the NBL for one season and the NBA for the next 15. The 6 ft 8 in forward made 15 NBA playoff appearances, averaging 19.2 points per game. Dolph was selected for 12 consecutive NBA All-Star games. During his career, he averaged 18.2 points per game, and he ended his brilliant basketball career 15th on the all-time scoring list with 19,249 points.

This Hall of Famer was a member of the Nats' NBA Championship team in 1955. He made the All-NBA First Team six times, led the league in rebounding in 1951, and led the NBA in free throw percentage for three years. He was named to the NBA 25th Anniversary All-Time Team.

Barney Sedran

Barney Sedran was graduated from DeWitt Clinton High School in New York City in 1907 and City College of New York in 1911. At 5ft 4in, he was judged too small to play on his high school team, so he played independent ball starring for CCNY. Sedran was the leading City College scorer for three years and was captain of the 1910 team. He was selected to many All-Star teams. Beginning in 1911, he played on ten championship professional teams over 15 years. In 1913 he scored goals from 25 to 30 feet on courts with no backboards. Sedran played with most of the major eastern professional teams including the Carbondale Salukis, who won 35 straight from 1914 to 1915. This Hall of Famer led the Fort Wayne Knights of Columbus team in 1923-24 and finished his playing career with the Cleveland Rosenblums from 1924 to 1926.

Right: *A 5ft 4in guard, Barney Sedran scored from far out on courts without backboards.*

Opposite: *Bill Sharman finishes a fast break. He led the NBA in free throw percentage for seven seasons.*

Bill Sharman

Did you know the only coach to win a championship in three different leagues also had a brilliant playing career? Bill Sharman coached a championship team in the NBA, ABA, and ABL. The two-time All-American was selected by the Washington Capitals on the second round out of the University of Southern California. The club folded halfway through the 1950-51 season and he was selected by Fort Wayne in the dispersal draft. He was immediately traded to the Boston Celtics.

He continued to play ten seasons with the Boston Celtics and made the playoffs every year, winning four championships. The 6ft 1in guard was one of the NBA's best foul shooters and had a lifetime free throw percentage of .883. He led the league for seven years in free throw percentage and set a record for that time with 55 consecutive free throws made (since broken by two players). In eight consecutive NBA All-Star games, he was named game MVP in 1955. He was named to the All-NBA First Team four times. Sharman finished his career as a player-coach in the American Basketball League as he led his team to the ABL crown. This Hall of Famer was named to the NBA 25th Anniversary All-Time Team.

Paul Silas

Paul Silas was one of only seven players to average over 20 points and 20 rebounds per game during his NCAA career at Creighton University (1961-64). He averaged 20.5 points and 21.6 rebounds per game. In 1963 he led the NCAA in rebounding with an average of 20.6 per game. He holds the college record for most rebounds in a three-year period with 1751.

St. Louis drafted him on the second round (12th pick) of the 1964 draft. In 15 NBA seasons, with six different teams, the journeyman averaged 9.4 points and 9.9 rebounds per game. The 6ft 7in forward was named to the All-NBA Defensive First Team twice, named to the All-NBA Defensive Second Team three times, and played in two NBA All-Star games. He was a member of the 1974 and 1976 Boston Celtics and the 1979 Seattle Supersonics World Championship teams. Silas was known best as a defensive and rebounding specialist.

Christian Steinmetz

Christian Steinmetz was graduated from South Division High School in Milwaukee in 1902 and the University of Wisconsin in 1905. He was a great two-sport captain in high school. Through his leadership and outstanding play, Steinmetz helped establish basketball as a recognized sport at Wisconsin and was to become known as the 'Father of Wisconsin Basketball.' At 5 ft 9 in he set five school records in 1905 that stood for well over 50 years: most points in a single game (50); most field goals in a single game (20); most free throws in a single game (26); most free throws in a single season (238); and most points in a single season (462). This Hall of Famer captained the team in 1905, was elected All-Western Conference, and became the first player to score over 1000 points in his college career. For 19 years he selected players to the All-Western Conference teams. He gained fame as one of his state's all-time athletic greats.

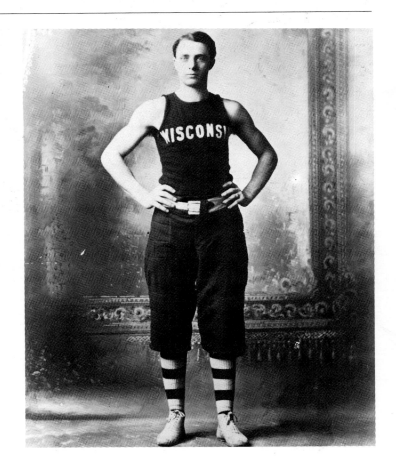

Opposite: *Paul Silas.*

Top left and right: *Silas was a splendid offensive rebounder who always got good position under the basket.*

Right: *Christian Steinmetz, a basketball pioneer in Wisconsin.*

Goose Tatum

Goose Tatum was the first great player-comedian. Back in 1942, the Harlem Globetrotters were considered the funniest team, but the best team was the Minneapolis Lakers. In 1948 Goose and the Trotters took them on and beat them 61-59, and beat them again in 1949.

In high school in Arkansas, baseball was Tatum's favorite sport. He attempted to make baseball his life by playing in the Negro League for the Cincinnati Clowns. His baseball skills were not good, but his comic antics made him a very popular player. In 1942 he was persuaded to try out for the Globetrotters, and during his 13-year Globetrotting career (1942-55) he established himself as the clown prince of basketball.

Goose provided something never seen in basketball before – laughter. He set the stage for the Globetrotters of today. More spectators have watched the Magicians of Basketball than any other team in basketball history. The Globetrotters have toured the world several times over. He had developed millions of fans before he died at the age of 45. Tatum's presence in the game of basketball will never be duplicated.

Isiah Thomas

In his first seven years of pro basketball, all with the Detroit Pistons, Isiah Thomas has helped revitalize the franchise. During those years, the Pistons went from one of the worst teams (21-61 in 1981) to the NBA Finals in 1988, where they were seconds away from being World Champions. Thomas gave a gutsy performance as he scored a playoff-career-high 43 points versus the Lakers, though he sprained his ankle during game six.

During his two-year college career at Indiana University (1980-81), he averaged 15.4 points per game. The 1981 All-American was a member of the NCAA Division I Championship team and was named the Tournament's Most Outstanding Player. He was a member of the 1980 U.S. Olympic team that boycotted the summer games.

The Pistons drafted him second in the 1981 draft as an undergraduate. Thomas was named to the All-NBA First Team three times and to the All-NBA Second Team twice. He has played in seven NBA All-Star games and was named game MVP in 1984 and 1986. The 6ft 1in guard has averaged 20.5 points per game and led the league in 1985 in assists. He is a flashy, steady performer. Thomas is the man the Pistons go to in a clutch situation.

Opposite: *Goose Tatum palmed the ball and performed many other tricks during 13 years as a Globetrotter.*

Right: *Isiah Thomas deftly gets rid of the ball as the defense closes in. He is at his best in the open court.*

Nate Thurmond

Nate Thurmond was the first player in NBA history to record a Quadruple Double: double figures in four categories during one game. Thurmond scored 22 points, had 14 rebounds, 13 assists, and 12 blocked shots in a 1974 game.

This All-American at Bowling Green State University averaged 17.8 points per game and holds an NCAA Tournament record for most rebounds in one game with 31. The 6 ft 11 in center was drafted on the first round by San Francisco. In 14 seasons, he was named to the 1964 All-NBA Rookie Team, made the All-NBA Defensive First Team twice, and the All-NBA Defensive Second Team three times. Thurmond was selected to play in seven NBA All-Star games, although due to injury he played in only five. During his professional career, he grabbed 14,464 rebounds, which places him fifth on the all-time list and includes an NBA record of 18 in one quarter. This Hall of Famer was a defensive wizard playing in an era of super centers. Thurmond was considered by many of his peers to be their toughest opponent.

Top left: *Nate Thurmond.*

Above: *Thurmond pulls down another one. He is fifth in career rebounds.*

Jack Twyman

Jack Twyman was an All-American and team captain at the University of Cincinnati, where he averaged 17.8 points per game. He led the Bearcats to a third-place finish in the NIT. The 6 ft 6 in forward was drafted with the tenth pick of the second round by the Rochester Royals. In 11 seasons with the Rochester/Cincinnati Royals, Twyman became the sixth player in NBA history to score 15,000 points. He played in six NBA All-Star games, had a career average of 19.2 points per game, led the NBA in field goal percentage in 1958, and was named to the All-NBA Second Team twice. This Hall of Famer was one of the greatest NBA shooting forwards, whose determination and leadership on and off the floor were as important to his team as his playing performance.

Above: *A savvy leader with a nice shooting touch, Jack Twyman averaged 19.2 points a game.*

Wes Unseld

Wes Unseld was a two-time All-American at the University of Louisville. During his college career, he averaged 18.9 rebounds and 20.6 points per game. In the 1968 draft, Unseld was drafted in the first round by the Baltimore Bullets with the second pick. He played 13 seasons, all with the Bullets organization, averaging 10.8 points and 13.9 rebounds per game. He is one of two players to be named NBA Most Valuable Player and Rookie-of-the-Year in the same season (the other is Wilt Chamberlain). This Hall of Famer was named to the 1969 All-NBA First Team, led the NBA in rebounding in 1975, and led the NBA in field goal percentage in 1976. This great team player and rebounder played in five NBA All-Star games and was named the Playoff MVP of the 1978 NBA Championship.

Right: *Wes Unseld.*

Below: *Unseld was known for his rebounding and quick outlet passes.*

Below right: *Unseld outmuscles Dave Robisch in 1980.*

Opposite: *Chet Walker was an All-Star seven times.*

Chet Walker

At Bradley University (1959-62), Chet Walker averaged 24.4 points per game in three years of varsity play. The two-time All-American was drafted by the Syracuse Nationals in the second round of the 1962 NBA draft. The Syracuse franchise transferred to Philadelphia in 1964, where he played six years, and then six more with the Chicago Bulls. He was named to the All-NBA Rookie Team, and was a member of the NBA Championship team in 1967. The 6 ft 7 in forward scored 18,831 points (18th on the all-time list) and averaged 18.2 points per game. In 105 playoff games, he averaged 18.2 points per game. Walker led the NBA in free throw percentage in 1971 and played in seven NBA All-Star games.

Bill Walton

Above: *A Bill Walton tip-in.*

At UCLA from 1971 to 1974 Bill Walton enjoyed one of the most successful college careers in the history of college basketball. The three-time Player-of-the-Year played in three NCAA Division I Final Fours, winning the 1972 and 1973 Championships. He won the Tournament's Most Outstanding Player award both times. Walton averaged 20.3 points and 15.6 rebounds per game. He holds the NCAA Tournament records for highest field goal percentage in one year with 76.3 and in a college career with 68.6.

The Portland Trailblazers drafted him with the number one pick in the 1974 draft. He was named to the 1977 All-NBA Second Team, named to the 1978 All-NBA First Team, named to the All-NBA Defensive First Team twice, and was named the 1978 NBA MVP. Walton has played in one NBA All-Star game. In 1977 he led the league in rebounding and blocked shots, won an NBA World Championship with Portland, and was named the NBA Playoff MVP. He shares the NBA Championship series game record for most blocked shots with eight. He played on a second World Championship team in 1986 with the Boston Celtics. He was the recipient of the 1986 NBA Sixth Man Award. The 6 ft 11 in center has averaged 13.3 points and 10.5 rebounds per game, despite an injury-plagued professional career. In 14 NBA seasons, Walton has played only 468 games out of a possible 1148.

Jerry West

Right: *Jerry West checks the score.*

Opposite: *The quintessential pressure player, West leads in playoff scoring average with 29.1 points a game. West was selected for the All-Star game in each of his 14 seasons.*

Jerry West, a two-time All-American at West Virginia University, averaged 24.8 points per game. He led his team to the runner-up position in the 1959 NCAA Tournament and was named the Tournament's Most Outstanding Player. In 1960, he co-captained the U.S. Olympic team to a gold medal.

The Minneapolis Lakers drafted him with their second pick in the 1960 NBA draft. That same year,

the Minneapolis franchise transferred to Los Angeles. The 6 ft 2 in guard had a brilliant 14-year career, all with the Lakers. West averaged 27 points per game and scored 25,192 points in 932 games, which places him sixth on the all-time scoring list. He was named to the All-NBA First Team ten times, named to the All-NBA Defensive First Team four times, led the league in assists in 1972, and led the NBA in scoring in 1970. He took the Lakers to the playoffs 13 out of his 14 years and played in nine NBA Finals, winning the 1972 NBA Championship. West was named the Playoff MVP in the 1969 Finals.

West is the NBA's all-time playoff leader in free throws made with 1213, and a scoring average of 29.1. He was selected to play in 14 NBA All-Star games and was named game MVP in 1972. This Hall of Famer always wanted the ball when the game was on the line, and he came through so consistently and so often that he earned the nickname 'Mr. Clutch.' He was named to the NBA 35th Anniversary All-Time Team.

Lenny Wilkens

At Providence College from 1957 to 1960, Lenny Wilkens averaged 14.9 points per game. The 1960 Second Team All-American was named the 1960 National Invitational Tournament (NIT) MVP as his team was runner-up. The St. Louis Hawks drafted him in the first round of the 1960 draft. In 15 NBA seasons, with four different teams, he scored 17,772 points (27th on the all-time points scored list) and had an average of 16.5 points per game. Wilkens is in the top ten of many of the NBA's career lists: second on most assists with 7211; tenth on most free throws made with 5394; ninth on minutes played with 38,064; and sixth on games played with 1077. He led the league in assists in 1970 and played in nine NBA All-Star games (MVP in 1971).

The 6 ft 1 in guard enjoyed his greatest success with St. Louis as he led them to the 1961 NBA Finals, where they lost to Boston. He was a player-coach for Seattle in 1970-72 and Portland in 1975. This Hall of Famer finally won a World Championship in 1979 as Seattle's coach. He is a master of the game and one of the greatest thinkers ever to wear a uniform. Wilkens has been a successful pro player and coach for 28 years.

Jamaal Wilkes

Jamaal Wilkes averaged 15 points in three seasons at UCLA (1971-74). The 1974 All-American was a member of the Bruins' 1972 and 1973 NCAA Division I Championship team. In college he was known as Keith Wilkes.

Golden State drafted him 11th in the first round of the 1974 draft. He went on to enjoy a successful 12-year career (three with Golden State, eight with the Lakers, and one with the Clippers). Wilkes was named the 1975 NBA Rookie-of-the-Year, named to the All-NBA Defensive Second Team twice, and played in three NBA All-Star games. As a rookie, he helped Golden State to its only NBA World Championship title. He signed as a free agent with the Lakers and became an integral part of five NBA Championship appearances, winning titles in 1980, 1982, and 1985.

The 6 ft 6 in forward had a career average of 17.7 points and a playoff average of 16.1 points per game. Wilkes went by the nickname 'Silk' because of his smooth style of play.

Right: *Jamaal Wilkes gets off a one-hander.*

Opposite: *Wilkes in traffic.*

Top: *Lenny Wilkens directs his team. Wilkens is second in career assists and played in nine All-Star games.*

Dominique Wilkins

Dominique Wilkins averaged 21.6 points per game during his college career at the University of Georgia (1980-82). The two-time Second Team All-American was drafted as the number three pick by Utah as an undergraduate. Before he ever put on a Utah uniform, he was traded to the Atlanta Hawks, where he became an immediate force in the NBA. In six NBA seasons, all with Atlanta, Wilkins has averaged 26.0 points per game. He is rapidly moving up on the career all-time points scored list. He was named to the 1983 All-NBA Rookie Team, named to the 1986 All-NBA First Team, and to the All-NBA Second Team twice. The 6 ft 8 in forward led in scoring in 1986 with an average of 30.3 points per game. He has participated in three NBA All-Star games. Wilkins is a dynamic player who has helped establish the Atlanta franchise as a team to be reckoned with.

Above: *Dominique Wilkins led the NBA in scoring with 30 points a game in 1986.*

Right: *Wilkins about to score on a lay-up.*

Opposite: *James Worthy, the 1988 Playoff MVP, has an explosive first step.*

James Worthy

James Worthy averaged 14.5 points per game during his college career at the University of North Carolina (1980-82). The 1982 All-American led the Tarheels to the NCAA Division I Championship as he was named the Tournament's Most Outstanding Player in 1982.

The Los Angeles Lakers drafted him number one as an undergraduate in the 1982 draft. In six NBA seasons with the Lakers, Worthy has lived up to his first-pick potential by averaging 17.4 points per game. He was named to the 1983 All-NBA Rookie Team, has made three NBA All-Star appearances, and was named the 1988 Playoff MVP. The 6ft 9in forward has played in five NBA Finals, winning the title in 1985, 1987, and 1988. He has a career playoff average of 20.7 points per game. In such a short period of time, Worthy has already accomplished what many players dream about.

THE 100 GREATEST BASKETBALL PLAYERS

BY RANK

1. Wilt Chamberlain
2. Kareem Abdul-Jabbar
3. Bill Russell
4. Larry Bird
5. Oscar Robertson
6. Earvin Johnson, Jr
7. Jerry West
8. Julius Erving
9. Bob Cousy
10. Rick Barry
11. Pete Maravich
12. George Mikan
13. Michael Jordan
14. Bob Pettit
15. Bobby McDermott
16. Elgin Baylor
17. Moses Malone
18. John Havlicek
19. Bob Davies
20. Jerry Lucas
21. Dolph Schayes
22. Elvin Hayes
23. Bob Lanier
24. Paul Arizin
25. Bill Walton
26. Sam Jones
27. Nate Thurmond
28. Alex English
29. Kevin McHale
30. Billy Cunningham
31. Dave Cowens
32. George Gervin
33. Gail Goodrich
34. James Worthy

35. Ed Macauley
36. Wes Unseld
37. Hank Luisetti
38. Joe Fulks
39. Isiah Thomas
40. Bob Kurland
41. Patrick Ewing
42. Nate Archibald
43. Dominique Wilkins
44. Adrian Dantley
45. Akeem Olajuwon
46. Dan Issel
47. Cliff Hagan
48. Bob McAdoo
49. Mark Aguirre
50. Dave DeBusschere
51. Charles Barkley
52. Willis Reed
53. Walt Bellamy
54. Walt Frazier
55. Clyde Lovellette
56. Bill Bradley
57. Earl Monroe
58. Jack Twyman
59. Dennis Johnson
60. Jamaal Wilkes
61. Hal Greer
62. George McGinnis
63. Bill Sharman
64. Lou Hudson
65. Calvin Murphy
66. Joe Lapchick
67. Dave Bing
68. K. C. Jones

69. Frank Ramsey
70. Barney Sedran
71. Paul Endacott
72. Johnny Beckman
73. Chet Walker
74. Tom Heinsohn
75. Laddie Gale
76. Artis Gilmore
77. Tom Gola
78. Benny Borgmann
79. Jim Pollard
80. Dutch Dehnert
81. Lenny Wilkens
82. Slater Martin
83. Bob Dandridge
84. Paul Silas
85. Al Cervi
86. Neil Johnston
87. Andy Phillip
88. Max Friedman
89. Danny Manning
90. John Russell
91. Charles Cooper
92. Kevin Porter
93. Nat Holman
94. Christian Steinmetz
95. Tom Barlow
96. Goose Tatum
97. John Roosma
98. Bevo Francis
99. Ann Meyers
100. Nancy Lieberman

Opposite: *When Wilt went to the basket, he was head and shoulders above the rest.*

INDEX

Numerals in *italics* designate illustrations